DATE DUE

GAYLORD			

John Barleycorn Must Die

John Barleycorn Must Die

The War Against Drink in Arkansas

Ben F. Johnson III

The University of Arkansas Press
Fayetteville
2005

09   08   07   06   05   5   4   3   2   1

Designed by Ellen Beeler

☺ The paper used in this publication meets the minimum requirements of the American National Standard for Permanence of Paper for Printed Library Materials Z39.48-1984.

Library of Congress Cataloging-in-Publication Data

Johnson, Ben F., 1953–
  John Barleycorn must die : the war against drink in Arkansas / Ben F. Johnson III.
    p. cm.
  ISBN 1-55728-787-2 (alk. paper)
  1. Temperance—Arkansas—History. 2. Prohibition—Arkansas—History.
  I. Title.
  HV5297.A8J64 2005
  363.4'1'09767—dc22

                                                                    2004021963

This project was made possible in part by support from the Old State House Museum and the Arkansas Natural and Cultural Resources Council.

Contents

Foreword

Ben Johnson proves in *John Barleycorn Must Die: The War Against Drink in Arkansas* that he is an indefatigable researcher, tenacious in ferreting out the details. His study of the war against demon rum is fascinating.

As the grandson of a circuit ridin', shoutin', whiskey hatin' Methodist preacher, and the son of a mother who was an active member of the Scott County Chapter of the Woman's Christian Temperance Union for 52 years until her death in 1982, I have always had a keen interest in prohibition and dry laws.

The county of my youth (Scott) was bone dry by law, but there were pockets of brewing and bootlegging scattered throughout the Ouachita Mountain region.

I spent the first fourteen years of my life—delightful years I might note—in the company-owned sawmill town of Forester (no longer in existence). The superintendent of the mill, W. A. McKeown, was a kindly man, but he was a devout Methodist, and was hard agin' spirituous liquors. Since he could fire you and order you out of your company-owned house in the same breath, his disdain for alcohol had a strong impact on the community. I never saw or heard of drinking in public—not even during the wild melee following the announcement of victory over Japan and the end of World War II.

The Scott County Chapter of the WCTU often met in the living room of our home during the '50s and '60s. As I recall the members wore a ribbon or pin as a symbol of membership. As a youngster, I would listen in on some of the meetings. They invariably discussed ways to fight wet laws and ways to discourage imbibing. Theirs was a "zero tolerance "concept. Meetings were laced with prayers for abstinence and for dry laws.

The WCTU officially went out of existence about 1985. Most of the members, including my mother, had crossed the River Jordan by this time—they would have been saddened by the demise.

I am satisfied that imbibing is much more acceptable to Arkansans today in general than it was in times past. Regardless of one's personal experience with John Barleycorn, this book doesn't take a position "fer or agin'" spirituous liquor, but it does help the reader to understand that, in earlier times, opposition to the sale and consumption was deep and wide.

Judge William R. Wilson
United States District Court,
Eastern District of Arkansas

Preface

John Barleycorn Must Die first emerged as an exhibit at the Old State House Museum (OSHM) in Little Rock from late 2003 through October 2005. I was the guest curator, charged with researching and writing the textual material seen by visitors to the OSHM gallery or to the interactive Web site.

As was the exhibit, this brief volume is a broad overview of the efforts to either moderate or halt drinking in Arkansas from the colonial era through recent disputes over the granting of private club licenses. In general, the state's antialcohol campaigns were popular movements that claimed the mantle of reform and acted in concert with national organizations. The opponents of prohibitionists included those who were generally suspicious of moral regulations as well as those who feared that banning drink would hobble economic and social modernization. The ebb and flow of the conflict revealed that Arkansans were full participants in a debate that reflected changing conditions and values throughout the country.

That Arkansas was caught up in a national crusade might surprise those who assume that the only battles over drink in the state were between federal revenue agents and moonshiners. I do not ignore the whiskey stills that were once found throughout the state, but they were less prevalent in Arkansas than in the southern Appalachians. Generally, local prohibitionists agitated more fervently against the open saloon than the hidden distillery. While the long-bearded mountain moonshiner may jostle against the severe, gaunt preacher among the stock images associated with the state, I hope that this casual history will make the case that the career of John Barleycorn in Arkansas is both more complex and interesting than suggested by the stereotypes.

I am deeply appreciative of Bill Gatewood, director of the Old State House Museum, for inviting me to serve as guest curator and for being willing to support the publication of this volume. The exhibit depended heavily upon the skills, patience, and experience of Jo Ellen Maack, curator, and Gail Moore, exhibit director, both of whom continued to locate and collect additional images for this book. Larry Ahart, OSHM historian, provided valuable insight and direction.

Readers of this volume owe much to Bettie Mahony of South Arkansas Community College, whose editorial revisions added clarity and removed clutter. I am grateful that Fred Williams of the University of Arkansas at Little Rock took the time to examine the manuscript for errors in fact and judgment. This task would have been harder without the consideration and aid of Andrea Cantrell and the staff at Special Collections, Mullins Library at the University of Arkansas, Fayetteville; Linda Pine and the staff at Special Collections, Ottenheimer Library at the University of Arkansas, Little Rock; and Marcia Crossman of the Arkansas United Methodist Archives at Bailey Library, Hendrix College. That I did not have to leave town quite so often in search of materials was due to the efforts of Donna McCloy and Peggy Walters of Magale Library, Southern Arkansas University.

I am also in debt to Susan Young of the Shiloh Museum of Arkansas History, and Charles Bolton of UALR, for offering expertise both personally and on the video that accompanied the exhibit. Robert Cowie of the Arkansas Historic Wine Museum set me straight on the history of winemaking in Arkansas. Clara Jones, Jenny Williams, and Don Williams generously reassured me that my drafts of the exhibit text panels were cogent and appropriate. Jerry Pyle, Tim Nutt, and Ethel Simpson very kindly directed my attention to valuable materials. Judge Bill Wilson deserves special mention for improving the manuscript, contributing to the exhibit video, and for kindly writing the foreword. I can only thank anonymously the person who supplied just enough moonshine to satisfy my research obligations.

I thank Southern Arkansas University for not only providing me work and first-rate colleagues but also for awarding research funds that made many things possible.

As with the biography of a troubled poet and the survey of modern Arkansas, Sherrel made this a better book than it otherwise would have been.

Whiskey Battles on the Arkansas Frontier

There were three men come out of the west
Their victory to try
And those three men took a solemn vow
John Barleycorn must die
They plowed, they sowed, they harrowed him in
Throwed clods upon his head
And those three men made a solemn vow
John Barleycorn was dead

RESOURCEFUL SUPPLIERS and defiant drinkers doomed the first prohibition policy in Arkansas. Only when community leaders judged alcohol a danger to order and social harmony did a ban take hold.

In 1766 the Quapaw Indians were skeptical about the new tenants of Arkansas Post. The Quapaws had formed a beneficial and profitable alliance with the French, who had established the Post in 1686 near the confluence of the Arkansas and White rivers. Following the French defeat in the Seven Years War, the Spanish acquired the French lands west of the Mississippi River and wished to exploit trading relations with the native peoples, including the Quapaws. Spanish diplomacy also aimed to check the British, colonial rivals with settlements across the Mississippi River from Arkansas. The British maneuvered to woo the Quapaws with a variety of trade goods, including rum. Spanish officials, on the other hand, refused to permit merchants to offer alcohol to the Indians.[1]

In 1768, Capt. Alexandre DeClouet explained to the governor in New Orleans that recent floods had left the Post without food stores and that the Quapaws demanded rum in exchange for corn. Unmoved, the governor urged the post commandant to persuade the Quapaws to forgo English liquor and advised him the following year to assemble the Indians for an address on "the evils of drink." Sermons seemed to have little effect. "Brilliant oratory, of which I am capable, hardly serves to content people of this color," DeClouet noted. Shortly afterward, the

Captain Alexandre DeClouet, commandant of Arkansas Post, failed to halt rum sales to the Quapaws.

COURTESY OF UNIVERSITY OF SOUTHWESTERN LOUISIANA.

commandant briskly asserted his authority by confiscating the liquor stock of a Post trader. Whatever qualms the Spanish had about private sellers, they were not hesitant to use alcohol as a tool of diplomacy. In 1771, Captain Fernando De Leyba entertained at his table a number of Quapaw chiefs and distributed fifty-seven bottles of brandy among their 350 followers. By 1779, regulation rather than prohibition was the rule. Post commanders compelled traders to secure a license before selling rum or brandy to the Indians. The Quapaws chafed under this paternalistic policy that did not cover other trade items.[2]

In 1779, Capt. Balthazar de Villiers decided in the interest of fairness and free trade to lift restrictions on provisioning liquor. The initiative was unpopular with post settlers, who anticipated unruly behavior from Indians. Captain Villiers acquiesced and confined alcohol distribution to only one site. Even the commandant's open market inclinations were tempered by his observation that the "passion for drink" led the "tribe to degenerate." In 1786, prominent Quapaw leaders, convinced that rum was disrupting village life, reversed course and requested that the Spanish interdict the trade. Only after the murder of a chief in a drunken brawl in the following year did the colonial governor outlaw the selling of liquor to the Quapaws.[3]

Europeans and the native peoples of colonial Arkansas forged close ties to sustain the fur trade and protect imperial boundaries. For United States political leaders, the 1803 Louisiana Purchase initially seemed an expansive wilderness, a suitable place to relocate the eastern Indian tribes resisting the expansion of the cotton economy in southern states. Even before the first political boundaries of Arkansas were drawn, Cherokee migrants responded to government incentives by settling in the region. Yet in the 1820s Cherokee and Choctaw leaders agreed to treaties surrendering land in Arkansas Territory for tracts in the Indian Territory to the west. Fort Smith, at the confluence of the Poteau and Arkansas rivers, represented the U.S. commitment to carrying out an orderly Indian removal policy. However, the trade in liquor once again preoccupied a commander at a outpost on the periphery of an empire.[4]

In early 1832, Lt. Gabriel Rains set up a sting operation to halt illicit trade with the Indians. The officer "employed a Choctaw Indian, assisted by two of his soldiers dressed in squaw's or Indian disguise" to purchase whiskey from a merchant in Belle Point, the settlement adjacent to Fort Smith. After the transaction was made, the soldiers hauled the proprietor before a county justice of the peace, who threw out the charges. Later that year, congressional legislation and war department regulations confirmed that whiskey found in the Indian territory must be seized as contraband. This federal action left the question of whether Indians could freely secure whiskey in Arkansas.[5]

In the summer of 1832, a federal grand jury in Little Rock highlighted the jurisdictional dilemma when it reported that "intemperance does exist to an unfortunate extent among all the Indians that have recently been removed to the west of Arkansas." Witnesses before the panel reported that of the six Belle Point mercantile houses huddled near the border, only one did not store "large quantities of whiskey." The jury blamed widespread drunkenness for numerous Indian deaths and for fort buildings catching fire on three occasions. While the jurors acknowledged that federal authority was "confined solely to transactions in Indian country," they cited a territorial law that appeared to give Arkansas officials the power to arrest and punish those who supplied "any spirituous, vinous, or other strong liquor" to the Indians.

Quapaw trading party, by Flery Generelly. Note figures drinking from bottles.

The jury was apparently referring to a statute enacted in May 1806 by the territorial government in St. Louis that would have applied at the time to the entire northern section of the original Louisiana Purchase. However, the law had been forgotten and was unenforceable.[6]

The argument that legal prohibition did not exist in Arkansas was underscored in a rejoinder to the Little Rock grand jury report published in the *Arkansas Gazette* and signed by twenty-two Belle Point businessmen. They conceded that local merchants sold whiskey to the Indians, but that "they have been, and still are, under the belief, that there is no law to prevent the sale of whiskey to Indians, any more than to whites, while within the limits of the territory." Capt. John Stuart, the new garrison commander, decided to leave the Belle Point taverns alone but mustered his soldiers to seize smugglers and liquor crossing into the Indian Territory. Stuart charged that Jonas Bigalow (a signer of the Belle Point letter in the *Gazette*) was one of the "most notorious" of the smugglers, but that he evaded capture by gaining inside information from corrupted soldiers. Stuart's complaints about whiskey sales to Indians were exceeded by his anger over the drinking habits of his own men. Paradoxically, the army allowed troops to frequent taverns even though Arkansas law made it illegal to sell alcohol to military personnel. Even if Stuart was of a mind to urge prosecution of soldiers, he knew that territorial judges would not enforce the ban. Eventually, Stuart blocked major smuggling routes along the Arkansas River, pushing the whiskey traders to make longer, more circuitous treks. In 1834, the War Department relocated the garrison ten miles to the north in hopes that troops could more easily surprise the Belle Point blockade runners.[7]

Most of the whiskey seeping into the Indian country was imported from manufacturers outside of Arkansas. In addition, whiskey brought upriver on keel boats remained a medium of exchange for thirsty hunters who harvested deer, otter, and bear skins. Nationally, by 1815 whiskey supplanted rum, the colonial drink of choice. The opening of new tracts of corn acreage in the Ohio River valley coupled with the lack of reliable transportation prompted farmers to distill their grain into alcohol to lower shipping costs. Cheap whiskey pushed American annual per capita alcohol consumption to five gallons, three times the modern rate. By 1830 midwestern farmers began to give up making corn whiskey as it became feasible to ship grain in bulk through the new network of canals. At the same time, commercial distilleries overwhelmed smaller operations and stabilized whiskey prices. Nevertheless, large sections of Arkansas throughout the antebellum era remained isolated from the national market, and homemade brew helped to oil the economy of the Bear State.[8]

Distillers set up dram shops to sell their wares or supplied taverns, which accommodated travelers with food and a bed. The editor of the *Arkansas Gazette* evidently knew his readers appreciated tips on whiskey-making. An 1828 article noted that John Gray of Georgia had learned by accident that tossing cotton seed into fermenting corn produced more whiskey without affecting the taste. These native manufacturing enter-

Trading post at Fort Smith on Indian Territory border.

COURTESY OF SPECIAL COLLECTIONS, UNIVERSITY OF ARKANSAS, LITTLE ROCK.

prises caught the attention of public officials. Facing an early fiscal crisis, the territorial legislature in October 1820 imposed a tax on distilleries and required grog shops and taverns to purchase licenses. The measure likely raised scant revenue since the preponderance of whiskey makers were little interested in marketing their wares. Friedrich Gerstäcker, a young German on an extended hunting trip in the late 1830s, observed that a distillery near the White River was a partnership in communal drinking by three young men rather than a source of profit.[9]

On the other hand, such ventures may have offered some African Americans rare entrepreneurial opportunities. On a cold and rainy November day Gerstäcker found refuge in an Ozark tavern: "Merry peals of laughter resounded from the well-lighted room, where a bright fire was blazing.... Three jovial looking fellows were sitting round it, telling stories, and roaring with laughter." One of the three was the distiller for the tavern, a "little fat man, with sparking eyes and ruby nose" who was "making constant love to the whiskey-bottle." The owner of the public house patronized by these white men, regaling the German with buffalo hunting stories, was "a free Negro."[10]

By the 1830s the growing middle class in the northeastern United States became increasingly alarmed by the violence and disorder erupting around unregulated taverns. In addition, the tradition of allowing workers in artisan shops to take a dram while on the job was disappearing due to demands for steadiness and efficiency in new factory settings. Anxieties over drinking were transformed into a social crusade by the national evangelical revival movement known as the Second Great Awakening. Just as the individual conversion experience was the aim of religious gatherings, temperance societies required their members to take the pledge to lead a new, sober life. The local associations affiliated with the American Temperance Society (formed in 1826) recruited upper and middle-class pillars of the community in the hopes their public abstemiousness would inspire others. While the temperance movement flourished in New England and the revivalist centers of western New York, it confronted formidable challenges when it infiltrated the southern states.[11]

Heavy drinking confirmed and dramatized the high status of south-ern leaders. Candidates for office were expected to "treat" the voters with generous portions of whiskey. Elected officials were feted with dinners during which supporters raised glass after glass to praise the victor's finer points. At an 1830 gathering in Little Rock, Ambrose Sevier, the Arkansas territorial delegate to Congress, was the subject of thirteen regular and forty-five volunteer toasts. Yet, widespread drunkenness clearly challenged elite dignity and power. William F. Pope described how a banquet in Little Rock to honor the U.S. commissioners who had negotiated a purchase of Cherokee lands in Arkansas degenerated into lowbrow brawl. The town worthies entertained the distinguished guests in a tavern on Main Street that attracted patrons from across the social spectrum. "After the banquet was over and the guests and more respectable portion of the company had retired from the hall, the tables were taken possession of by a lot of rowdies who were in a state of drunkenness bordering on frenzy, and made the hall resound with their oaths and yells." One of the revelers climbed onto one of the long tables and began marching forward, "kicking dishes, plates, glasses, and other articles of tableware in all directions." When he was pulled from the table, the young man stabbed another man to death and then escaped amid the confusion.[12]

If elite plantation owners recoiled at taking the temperance pledge, they wielded abstention as another tool to manage their labor force. As early as 1828, the territorial legislature allowed Little Rock to ban alco-hol sales to slaves lacking their owners' explicit permission, and in 1853 a similar measure carrying heavy fines and imprisonment was enacted to cover the entire state. The 1853 assembly also enjoined taverns from employing African Americans, whether free or slave. While this act reflected the state's obsession with trying to control the black popula-tion, it also curbed the prerogatives of owners and was probably disre-garded. In fact, reports reveal that in the late 1850s slaves worked in taverns in Camden and Van Buren.[13]

Temperance also aroused the ire of frontier citizens living at some distance from the emerging plantation regions in Arkansas. In these places seemingly far from heaven, camp meetings broke the isolation

Facing page:
Artist's conception of
1830s backwoods tavern.

DRAWING BY BILL REAMES.
COURTESY OF OLD STATE HOUSE
MUSEUM.

and encouraged women to become active in shaping the moral life of the settlements. The hard sayings of Methodist circuit riding ministers, those outriders of the Second Great Awakening, left no doubt that pouring out whiskey was God's work. Predictably, a reform threatening a basic economic activity and the liberty of backwoods freeholders drew few beyond the aggressively devout. This skepticism is replete in the writings of Charles F. M. Noland, the popular humorist whose fictional alter ego, Pete Whetstone, lived on the Devil's Fork of the Little Red River and dabbled in politics when not hunting. In a letter dated May 8, 1837, "Whetstone" recounted that a political opponent had gone among "the religious women" to report on his gambling and drinking. "Lawyer McCampbell says Pete's a sinner. He tells a lie: Pete loves God, fears the devil, and hates snakes. . . . He doesn't horse race, except for fun, and when there is a sure chance to win. He doesn't drink liquor except bald face whiskey, just to encourage our own 'stil houses."[14]

The towns were a different matter. Here resided the Arkansas business and professional class. These families were able to attend church services regularly but also were confronted by the mayhem spilling from the saloons. Order was more highly prized even in small urban centers than in the backwoods. Through both general legislation and municipal incorporation acts, state lawmakers permitted towns to regulate taverns and, in some cases, halt liquor sales within their precincts. By the 1830s the governing board of Little Rock had the power to ban gambling from drinking houses as well as punish those selling alcohol without a license. However, such regulations did not suppress public turmoil arising from strong drink. Throughout the 1830s Little Rock hosted a grand public barbecue each Fourth of July during which "people with bottles or jugs of whiskey went about offering it to all present." Sober-minded town dwellers believed an example needed to be set.[15]

By 1835, the American Temperance Society (ATS) boasted of eight thousand local associations and 1.5 million members throughout the nation. The presence of the ATS in Arkansas represented the strongest link between the southern frontier and the modernizing sections of the nation. Reflecting the ecumenical spirit of the Second Great Awakening, the Little Rock Temperance Society in 1831 first met at a Baptist church and selected as its president the Rev. William Stevenson, one of the pioneer organizers of the early territorial Methodist circuits. In general, Methodists were the most ardent for the cause, while the Baptists remained lukewarm until after the Civil War. The constitution of the Little Rock society included the standard pledge that required members to give up "all kinds of distilled spirits." At this point, the ATS permitted the tippling of beer and wine, which were thought to be less injurious and less prone to abuse. The Little Rock association also followed the national practice of opening membership to "persons of both sexes," marking the first opportunity for Arkansas women to engage in a public movement. Temperance organizations emerged in other communities

Brewing whiskey on the southern frontier.

LIBRARY OF CONGRESS, PRINTS AND PHOTOGRAPHS DIVISION.

although their pledges followed the ATS shift toward "teetotalism" or the abjuring of all alcoholic beverages. In 1842, the Clarksville society reported three hundred members, while one hundred had joined the newly organized Fort Smith association. Nearly all the candidates for political office in Phillips County that year had flocked to the "Total Abstinence Society" and promised not to ply the voters with liquor.[16]

Since the reputation of the temperance societies depended upon the discipline of those who took the pledge, they were vulnerable to derision when members fell off the wagon or offended moral sensibilities in other ways. True to their religious origins, the societies held public trials of those accused of backsliding. In 1843, the board of the Fayetteville Temperance Society expelled W. T. Larremore who "confessed that he had drunk WINE, which was proved by witnesses to be intoxicating liquor." Already in 1841 the society had been rocked when William McKnight Ball, vice president of the society, fled to Texas after it was revealed the Fayetteville branch of the state bank had come up short twenty thousand dollars under his management. In spite of such lapses, the society claimed credit for enlisting the support of three-quarters of the Fayetteville adult population.[17]

As the temperance movement matured, alcohol consumption in the United States declined. Yet, continued public drunkenness was an affront to the millennial expectations of the anti-alcohol reformers and prompted some to throw over "moral suasion" in favor of prohibition through coercion. Not surprisingly, the "no-license" strategy to halt the operation of local taverns took root in New England reform circles but also sprouted in southern states such as Tennessee, South Carolina, and Georgia.[18]

In an October 1842 letter in the *Arkansas Gazette,* William Stevenson, on behalf of the Little Rock Temperance Society, requested that the state's societies unite to pressure the legislature to stopper demon rum: "We intend . . . to petition for the repeal of all laws and parts of laws authorizing the licensing of the sale of alcohol in any quantity, from the dram up to a thousand gallons, or even ten thousand." Stevenson argued that such a measure was necessary to protect "our national rights as citizens," and compared its purpose to that of other laws that proscribed behaviors that endangered peace and safety. "But what are the evils of lotteries and Bowie knives, pistols and blacklegs, when compared with the evils of drunkenness?" In the previous year William Woodruff, the editor of the *Gazette,* had joined with temperance leaders to sponsor a large rally and Main Street parade, but he refused to justify the antiliquor cause according to "national rights" at a time when northern antislavery advocates condemned the southern labor system as incompatible with American democracy. In a subsequent editorial, Woodruff held that alcohol was the "potent, remorseless, and successful enemy of morality" rather than a threat to an individual's right to be secure. Endorsing the abolition of the saloon by government fiat uncomfortably echoed the calls for the abolition of slavery. As an alternative to prohibition of retail sales, Woodruff advocated a sizeable increase in the license fees on tavern owners and grocers who sold liquor. Neither a no-license act nor exorbitant fees, however, gained legislative approval.[19]

Robert Earnheart, a nineteenth-century corn farmer, operated a commercial distillery in the White River bottoms of Independence County.

COURTESY OF THE OLD INDEPENDENCE REGIONAL MUSEUM.

In 1851 the antebellum prohibition crusade secured a victory in Maine, which halted both the manufacture and sale of alcohol statewide. Thirteen states followed, although Delaware was the only slave state to take this path. Arkansas lawmakers continued to view the liquor question as a local matter. During the decade the state General Assembly approved the incorporation of a number of private academies with provisions forbidding the sale of alcohol within a prescribed distance of the school, usually two to three miles. An 1855 revision of the local license law offered local citizens the means to restrict dram shops for the first time. Under the measure, a person wishing to open a tavern had to submit to the county court a petition of support signed by the majority of the voters in the township where the business was to be located. In the following year, lawmakers authorized a local option election process. The act stipulated that voters in three Washington County townships were to decide in a special February 1857 election whether to allow the sale of liquor in any amount and that the question would appear on the local ballots in subsequent general elections. These 1850s measures introduced the core provisions that became the basis of antiliquor legislation following the Civil War.[20]

As Arkansas adopted laws similar to those approved in other states, a state chapter of a new national society recruited an ambitious set of men. By the mid-1840s, economic hard times and dissension over its teetotalism policy dissolved the American Temperance Society. Other groups arose to keep the crusade alive. The Sons of Temperance, founded in New York City, proved to be the antidrink organization that captured southern allegiance. A disproportionate percentage of the Sons' white membership resided in the slave states. (The organization did not enroll African Americans, but did have an auxiliary Daughters of Temperance led by women only.) In 1851 the Arkansas General Assembly approved the incorporation of the state division of the Sons of Temperance and recognized Samuel A. Sanders as the "Grand Worthy Patriarch." The Sons of Temperance was a fraternal organization that developed unique rituals and organized a mutual benefit association, a type of insurance program providing aid in times of illness. These bonds of support meant that individuals did not have to rely simply on their own self-discipline to stay dry. In addition, the secrecy surrounding the group's activities insulated backsliders and the organization from ridicule by nonmembers. As in northern states, town-dwelling artisans—blacksmiths, carpenters, cabinet-makers, printers, and shoemakers—represented a substantial presence on rolls of the southern wing of the Sons of Temperance. However, the rarity of such occupations in the frontier south left temperance with a small constituency.[21]

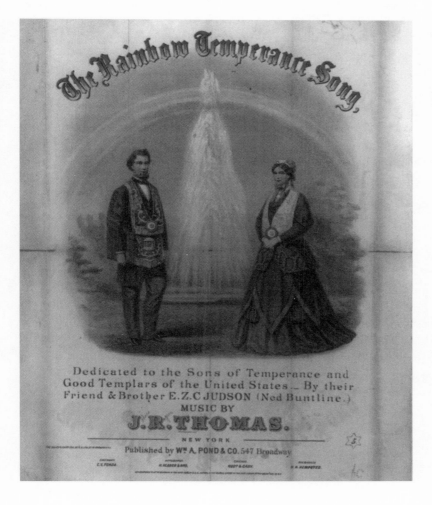

The Sons of Temperance organization also formed a women's auxiliary.

John Barleycorn continued to thrive in antebellum Arkansas, whether in defiance of local regulations or with the blessings of the law. Sam Williams recalled that around 1854 one of the two local gin mills closed when Washington in Hempstead County halted the sale of drinks. The other one underwent renovations. Peter O. Cox, the owner, hired a carpenter to board up the saloon bar and then cut small compartments into the new wall. Each compartment opening had a flat, horizontal wooden wheel, half of which remained hidden behind the partition. Each compartment bore a label indicating various popular drinks such as straight whiskey, a whiskey toddy, port, or brandy. "When the tippler walked into the place all he had to do to quench his thirst was to lay a dime in the little compartment bearing the name of the beverage he hankered after, giving the mysterious wheel a turn with the finger and presto!—in a moment the little wheel would come spinning back and minus the coin, but laden with his favorite tipple." No conversation passed through the bar partition, and no customer could give evidence against the person who supplied the drink.[22]

Those in the rising urban class in Arkansas concluded chronic intoxication retarded the state's progress and damaged its reputation. In 1851 John Keet arrived to keep the books for a general store in the notorious Mississippi River port of Napoleon. Travelers were of one mind that Napoleon was the nastiest, most vile sinkhole along the length of the river. In a letter to his uncle in Ireland, Keet revealed the shock of a skilled, ambitious young man encountering a raw, unformed society: "In fact, the Southern Americans are different from the Northern a great deal.... They have not the same steady, sober, peaceable, persevering & enterprising character possessed by their northern brethren.... Drinking is their principal, I might say their only enjoyment. And O! how strong drink degrades a people—turns them from men to imbeciles & demons, by turns.... The intemperate habits of the people here, form my principal objection to the place."[23]

While the growing influence of forces touting sobriety and discipline suggested the birth pangs of a developing economy and society, the temperance crusade faltered during the crisis that led to the Civil War.

The Law and White Lightning

Federal agents and local law enforcement
authorities searched for whiskey-still operations
in the most remote sections of Arkansas. Wishing
to dramatize their successes and to discourage
moonshiners, lawmen posed alongside captured
stills before destroying them.

*A large Newton County
still in a building
constructed against a
rock overhang.*

COURTESY OF *NEWTON COUNTY
TIMES*/SHILOH MUSEUM OF
OZARK HISTORY.

Law officers discover a Miller County still.

COURTESY OF SPECIAL COLLECTIONS, UNIVERSITY OF ARKANSAS, LITTLE ROCK.

A crowd gathers at a public burning of whiskey in Fayetteville.

COURTESY OF BOB BESOM/ SHILOH MUSEUM OF OZARK HISTORY. J. H. GORSUCH, PHOTOGRAPHER.

A five-hundred-gallon still found near a school, October 1925.

COURTESY OF TONY PERRIN.

Randolph County officers with a dismantled still, 1926.

COURTESY OF TONY PERRIN.

Gov. Harris Flanagan failed to enforce the ban on whiskey production in Confederate Arkansas.

From Civil War to Moonshine Wars

2

They let him lie for a very long time
'Til the rains from heaven did fall
And little Sir John sprung up his head
And so amazed them all,
They let him stand til the midsummer's day
'Til he looked both pale and wan
And Little Sir John's grown a long, long beard
And so became a man.

I N 1862, the Confederate state government of Arkansas enacted the first statewide restriction on liquor when it banned distilleries to conserve grain as well as sugar and molasses during the war. In contrast to the prewar measures, the act targeted manufacturing rather than the selling of spirits. Overwhelmed by greater challenges and without resources, officials could not bring to justice those eyeing large profits from a popular commodity. Ten stills made the community of Brownstown a magnet for soldiers and civilians alike. David Walker, the noted political leader and jurist, let it be known that he was willing to meet "any price in or out of reason" to obtain whiskey. Finally, in 1864, Gov. Harris Flanagan, also a reputed imbiber, acknowledged that the willingness of distillers to pay fines to stay in business rendered the law worthless.[1]

Temperance had better friends in the Republican-dominated state government and federal agencies during the Reconstruction era. Generally, antiliquor activists became Republican because of the party's principles endorsing individual enterprise, government activism on behalf of social betterment, and the benefits of a self-reliant work force. Northern reformers entering the defeated Confederate states after the war saw temperance as a way to promote the transition of the emancipated slaves from bondage to free labor. Before the reestablishment of state governments, agents for the Bureau of Refugees, Freedmen, and Abandoned Lands (Freedmen's Bureau) provided immediate relief to displaced southerners, enforced contracts setting out the terms of labor for former slaves, and built schools. The Bureau also founded temperance societies. In Arkansas societies in Lewisville, Washington, Little Rock, Helena, and Camden grew rapidly as hundreds of African Americans attended the weekly meetings. The Bureau's state head of education programs organized temperance schools attended by black children after Sunday church services. African American leaders clearly believed that eschewing drink was an avenue to prosperity as well as a means to disprove white assumptions that ex-slaves could not meet the demands of freedom. Religion confirmed the virtues of abstinence. The Second Great Awakening revival movement that had stoked early temperance fervor had also led to the widespread Christianization of the Southern slaves during the early nineteenth century. Independent black denominations quickly took root in the south after the Civil War, and temperance was incorporated into sermons expressing optimism about the future. At an 1868 gathering organized in Little Rock by the African Methodist Episcopal church, children sang tunes celebrating the importance of education as well as a song entitled "Downfall of Old King Alcohol."[2]

Seeking to modernize balloting procedures and wishing to minimize Democratic manipulation, Republican lawmakers established the practice of closing taverns on election day. On the other hand, the paternalistic impulse to regulate the moral life of African Americans frayed under the demands for equal treatment under the law. The landmark 1873 state civil rights statute that outlawed various forms of discrimination in public accommodations also set punishment for those who refused to sell alcohol to any person "on account of race or color." Saloon keepers apparently resisted serving black customers, and the law did little to disturb the usual social arrangements. Still, R. A. Dawson, an African American state senator, made a successful complaint against a white saloon owner, who was fined for refusing to serve him. In 1875 Charles Nordhoff, the noted New York reporter, described a somewhat fluid racial system in which some establishments had separate bars for white and black customers while men of both races drank alongside one another in other saloons. As events unfolded, the 1873 legislative session was the final one before the Democratic party retook control of state government and brought to an end Arkansas Reconstruction. Civil and political rights began to erode as the planters sought to regain control of black labor. The U.S. government was unwilling to intervene after 1876 to ensure equality and liberty for those emancipated in the terrible war. On the other hand, the authorities did not flinch at using force to collect the federal excise taxes on liquor. In Arkansas, as elsewhere in the region, the moonshine wars flared after Reconstruction.[3]

The first national internal tax (as opposed to tariffs) was the 1791 excise on distilled whiskey. This measure provoked the famous "Whiskey Rebellion" by Pennsylvania farmers, who quickly dispersed with the arrival of an army led by President George Washington. In 1802 the administration of Thomas Jefferson repealed the excise, but it was revived to meet the costs of the War of 1812. The return of peace buried the levy, and Americans paid no internal taxes until the Civil War. To defray the expense of the Union military mobilization, the Tax Act of 1862 not only authorized an array of taxes, including the first income tax as well as new excises on distilled spirits and malt beverages, it also created the Office of the Commissioner of Internal Revenue. By 1883 most of the war-era taxes were repealed, but the excise on alcohol and the requirement that distillers obtain a federal license survived. The Bureau of Internal Revenue, as it was informally known, appointed in each state a district collector, who, in turn, hired deputy collectors. The deputy collectors and the special deputies employed on a per diem basis to assist in raids on illegal stills were the "revenuers" of rural lore.[4]

Small distillers had largely ignored antebellum Arkansas tax and license measures. This easy evasion of regulations vanished with the end of the Old South. The arrival of agents enforcing federal laws carrying stiff prison sentences for violators transformed a domestic craft into a hazardous occupation. If travelers in Arkansas before the Civil War could have happened upon distilleries along public thoroughfares, the new moonshine operations huddled near isolated creeks. The incentive for most moonshiners was clearly economic. As backwoods farmers became caught up in the market economy, they faced steadily declining crop prices throughout the late nineteenth century. At the same time, the penetration of the upland sections and river bottoms by railroad lines brought in increasing numbers of thirsty loggers and sawmill workers. In the 1890s a southern farmer could make about ten dollars when he hauled his twenty bushels of corn to town, whereas distilling forty bushels into 120 gallons of whiskey could clear $150, without the federal tax.[5]

Moonshine was also attractive because one could easily learn the basic process. While it was possible to use materials at hand such as a

Rudimentary moonshine still operation.

COURTESY OF ARKANSAS HISTORY COMMISSION.

wash pot and a used barrel, the enterprising moonshiner understood that good whiskey could not be made without a first-rate still. Throughout Arkansas certain craftsmen were noted for forging state-of-the-art copper stills. Unlike other metals, copper would not leave an aftertaste. From the top of the still jutted an elbow-shaped pipe that tapered from four inches to about one inch in diameter. Attached to the end of this outlet was a twenty-foot coiled copper pipe known as the "worm," which was looped inside an adjacent barrel kept full of cold water during distillation of the sour mash. Moonshiners set up near creeks and rivers to assure a ready supply of water. All whiskey came from sour mash, but recipes varied. Commonly, the moonshiner mixed corn meal and hot water in separate "mash barrels," later adding large scoops of sugar as well as yeast. After two days the fermenting mixture began to bubble furiously and continued to do so for several days. When the mash quit "working," it had the "kick of a mule colt" and was ready to be transferred to the still.

As the moonshiner stoked the wood fire under the still, the alcohol vapor rose to the top and then condensed into liquid as it passed through the coiled worm submerged in the cooling barrel. A potent rivulet trickled from the end of the worm into waiting half-gallon fruit jars. "You could only run a stream a little larger than a pencil," recalled a Columbia County moonshiner. Lowering the fire reduced the stream. The first jars were high proof while the adulterated end of the batch was known as "singlings" or "low wine." The low wine was set aside, poured back into the still, and cooked again. Once more, the strong first drops were followed by a flow of decreasing proof. "We always ran the low wine down to where you could pour some of it in the fire and if it flashed up we would keep on running. If it put the fire out like water, we would quit," noted the south Arkansas distiller.[6]

In 1876, as military units withdrew from southern states, a new national revenue commissioner launched a crackdown on moonshiners. Causalities on both sides of the law mounted as the prospect of federal prison sentences hardened the resolve of whiskey makers to avoid arrest. The agents came to identify moonshiners in certain states by their method of resistance. The Georgians were counted on to run while the

Kentucky distillers engaged in open battle. Those in Arkansas waited in ambush. However, not all the perils to the federal officials were confined to the whiskey hollows. Local officials arrested revenue agents for injuring moonshiners but lightly punished individuals who wounded or killed the officers carrying out their duties. Between 1876 and 1879, southern state courts prosecuted 165 agents for actions taken against still operators. In the summer of 1897, a federal deputy marshal and two other members of a posse approached a large still in Searcy County located "in a deep ravine protected on the lower side by a fort built of logs and stone." The marshal's call for the surrender of the wildcatters (moonshiners) was answered by gunfire from a porthole in the fort's wall. The wounded marshal tried to use the body of a dead compatriot as a shield but was dispatched by another shot. After a trial in the Russellville circuit court, the killer was given a six-month sentence.[7]

The hostility of local and state officials toward the collectors indicates that moonshiners relied upon the silence and protection of neighbors. On the other hand, the violence associated with the operations increasingly disturbed those in the urban middle class who wanted to launch their communities into a new social and economic direction. In 1898 John Burris, a legendary deputy collector credited with destroying 150 stills in little over a year, investigated moonshining in Cleburne County in response to entreaties from "the best citizens in the adjoining counties." Posing as a timber buyer, Burris located three stills near the village of Hiram before returning to Little Rock to secure warrants and a posse. The ensuing raid succeeded in destroying three stills and capturing six wildcatters, but Burris and his men were forced to swim the Little Red River to evade fifteen moonshiners in pursuit. Understanding that whiskey-making pervaded the county, Burris soon communicated through an elderly justice of the peace that the U.S. government was prepared to bring in larger forces to suppress moonshining unless the distillers first accepted an offer of amnesty. Burris and one other officer, after receiving assurances of cooperation, returned to the locale from which they had recently fled: "All that evening wagons continued to arrive on the streets of Hiram loaded with copper stills and men, and when night came there were seventeen stills and forty-seven voluntary prisoners."[8]

Large-scale raids netting mass arrests tested the diplomacy and inge-
nuity of the officers transporting the wildcatters through hostile territory. In early 1898 Burris shepherded twenty-three prisoners toward Hot
Springs following a seven-day campaign through remote Scott County.
Understanding that he could not rely on local citizens for shelter and
hot meals, Burris chose his camping sites in advance. Upon reaching

*Isaac Stapleton was a
federal revenue agent
and historian of the early
Arkansas moonshine wars.*

COURTESY OF OLD STATE
HOUSE MUSEUM.

Hot Springs, he ensconced his charges in the Great Northern Hotel. This was the first visit to a city of any size for nearly all the prisoners, and "one man fainted while going up in the elevator." The following day Burris herded the moonshiners on a train to Fort Smith, where several were sentenced to the federal penitentiary at Leavenworth, Kansas.[9]

Moonshining persisted well into the twentieth century and expanded as prohibition measures forced all those who purchased liquor to do business with lawbreakers. In the process, the bloodshed and corruption associated with the stills faded from the popular mind. The image of brewing corn liquor was tamed into a traditional craft practiced by mountain folk keeping the modern world at bay. This alteration in the reputation of wildcatters resulted, in part, from sympathetic portrayals by the collectors of Ozark folklore and from the general discrediting of temperance following the repeal of national Prohibition in 1933.

Otto Ernest Rayburn, one of the more notable shapers of the romance of the Ozarks, believed that the wildcatter was no different from other hill dwellers in meeting the dismissal of outsiders with resigned self-effacement. Rayburn observed in his *Ozark Country* (1941), "Many law-abiding citizens wink at the idea of liquor enforcement in the backhills, and 'revenuers' are as unpopular with hillsmen as ticks with tourists." The writer's unpublished "Folk Encyclopedia" manuscript, however, noted that as the Ozarks began to resemble other places, the moonshiner was "persecuted by press and pulpit, chased by the law, and held in contempt by the righteous public." Charles Morrow Wilson, in a 1959 collection of reminisces, quoted a lecture by an experienced moonshiner that fused the touted Ozark practicality with antitemperance feeling: "Human kind is a drinkin' kind. Me and Alfred plants our corn, raises it shucks it and takes it to mill and gets it mealed. If my woman goes and makes a pone of bread, that don't violate no law. Then why shouldn't we put part of our crop to licker?...Honest licker is bound and beholden to come out a crop. And back in these parts hit's our only chance for a fair crop."[10]

Ozark romanticism obscured some facts about moonshining in Arkansas. While the smoke from stills could be spied throughout the upland south, Arkansas during the moonshine era could lay claim to far fewer wildcat whiskey operations than the Appalachian regions. And other sections of the state were as remote as the northern hills and as promising for distillers. The islands in the Mississippi River, floating between state jurisdictions, were ideal sites for "blind tigers," illegal saloons that sold bootlegged and moonshine whiskey to Delta farmers and workers. In 1896, George Wilson, "whose house-boat was well-stocked with liquor in pint, half pint and quart bottles," did business from Dawson's Landing, fifty miles south of Helena. Customers thirsting for the renowned "Ike Williams, Pure Old Panther Piss" had to find Williams on Island 34, where they purchased five-gallon jugs and fifty-gallon kegs sporting labels with a graphic illustration.[11]

Ozark residents and a Newton County still.

COURTESY OF JIM HENDERSON/ SHILOH MUSEUM OF OZARK HISTORY.

The early 1920s oil discoveries in south Arkansas created raucous boomtowns shortly after national Prohibition was enacted. Ernest Pyle, who was a wildcatter in Punkin Center in southern Columbia County, recalled that with the enactment of the Eighteenth Amendment, "moonshine whiskey broke out all over this country. Most everybody got involved in some way or another." Greater numbers of illegal distillers meant that those in the customarily isolated locations operated at a disadvantage. Pyle explained, "I lived too far off of the main roads. There was always somebody selling whisky before they got to my house, and the whisky drinkers would stop and get their whiskey before they got to me." Yet, in areas remote from banks and town stores, corn liquor was recognizable currency. "I did trade a lot of whisky for some things that I needed like geese, fruit jars, tools, fence wire, barbed wire, guineas, guns, pea seeds, and cotton seed. I even swapped whisky for two cars," recalled Pyle.[12]

Most moonshiners continued to take pains to escape scrutiny. In 1921, O. C. Pill promised a Smackover club owner that he could brew better whiskey than what the proprietor had been paying him to haul from Oklahoma. Although he had little experience making alcohol, Pill and a partner took the first step when they chose an almost inaccessible site on Fish Trout Lake in southeastern Union County. They sent for a coppersmith from Little Rock who specialized in stills and hired him to construct one "as big as the Henry H. Cross Refinery." Pill set up a permanent camp at the still site, where he also relocated his wife and mother-in-law. He then met the challenge of distribution by constructing a power boat large enough to carry six ten-gallon kegs to the Calion port on the Ouachita River. As promised, the club owner paid Pill eight dollars for each gallon of whiskey, which was loaded at the dock onto trucks for the journey to Smackover. Finally, Pill reduced the riskiest aspect of his enterprise by bribing law officers in both Union and Ashley counties. Local police and deputies usually were among the first to know of a planned federal raid. "Internal Revenue shook us down twice and didn't find a thing. We knew they was coming the day before," boasted Pill.[13]

The WCTU Crusade Against the Saloon

Founded in 1876, the Arkansas Woman's Christian Temperance Union was a significant vehicle for women's political and social activism in the era before the vote was won. Members insisted that the death of the saloon would protect children and save men from themselves.

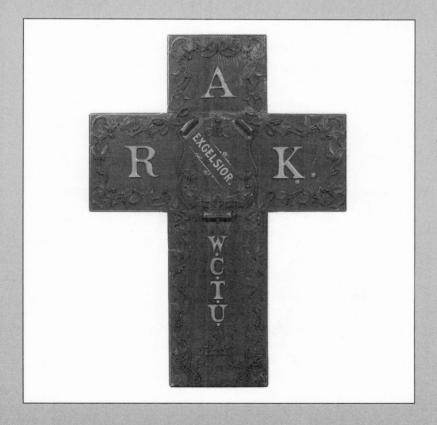

In 1902, students of the state school for the deaf constructed a cross that was presented to the state WCTU.

COURTESY OF OLD STATE HOUSE MUSEUM.

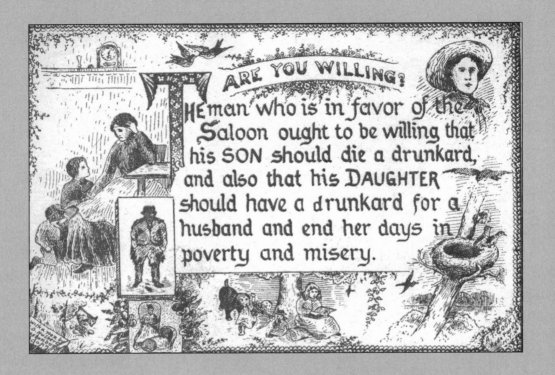

WCTU literature
emphasized that liquor
was a root cause of an
array of social problems.

The WCTU organized
a children's auxiliary and
promoted temperance
education.

WCTU poster revealing that modern technology extended liquor's destructive potential.

COURTESY OF OLD STATE HOUSE MUSEUM.

GASOLINE +
ALCOHOL =
DANGER

NO INTOXICATING DRINKS SOLD TO MINORS

WCTU painting depicting a bucolic, alcohol-free scene.

COURTESY OF OLD STATE HOUSE MUSEUM.

Carry Nation's tactics and notoriety troubled national WCTU leaders, although Arkansas temperance activists welcomed her move to Eureka Springs.

Prohibition Armies March to Victory

They hired men with the scythes so sharp to cut him off at the knee
They rolled him and tied him around the waist and served him
barbarously
They hired men with the hard pitchfork
To pierce him through the heart
And the loader he has served him worse than that
For he bound him to a cart
They wheeled him round and around the field 'til they came unto a barn
And these three men made a solemn oath on poor John Barleycorn

THE MOONSHINE WARS in the late nineteenth century on occasion claimed collateral victims. In 1876 four Methodist preachers traveling home from a general council meeting made a stopover in an Ozark village near Russellville. Suspicious that the unfamiliar visitors were revenuers, local moonshiners shot three of the clergymen, one of whom died the following day. Such incidents deepened the convictions of antialcohol proponents that drink endangered not only the imbiber. Of course, the prohibitionists did not want simply to stamp out illegal liquor production; they wanted to make all liquor illegal. In fact, national temperance organizations had denounced the 1862 federal tax measure that was the basis of the revenue battles against moonshiners because it appeared to give official sanction to drink. The failure of the temperance lobby to kill the tax law reflected a general decline in its influence as the pre-Civil War state prohibition laws fell by the wayside and

The first women's crusades against saloons were spontaneous and often effective.

saloons operated in dry precincts with the cynical tolerance of local officials. In the intensely competitive politics of the late nineteenth century, neither Democratic nor Republican leaders wanted to embrace an issue that would alienate key constituencies. One group of Americans excluded from the electoral process seized the opportunity to mount a new type of campaign to turn up the heat on wary politicians. In the winter of 1873, women in Ohio towns marched on saloons and stood outside singing hymns and praying until the owners signed a pledge to stop serving drinks. Before it ended the following year, this "Woman's Crusade" reached 912 communities in 31 states and gave birth to the Woman's Christian Temperance Union (WCTU).[1]

Founded in Cleveland, Ohio, in November 1874, the WCTU under its first president, Annie Wittenmeyer, adopted the Crusaders' approach of converting drunkards and shaming liquor retailers but shrank from public demonstrations in front of saloons. Significantly, at its first convention the Union determined not to enroll men. This decision would lead the WCTU to become the largest and most influential women's organization in the United States before the twentieth century. Historians have noted that while temperance was a moral reform movement surging out of evangelical churches, the cause resonated particularly with women, who understood too well that male drinking endangered the physical safety and financial security of wives and children. The fight against the saloon united conservative women who insisted they were fulfilling their roles as defenders of the home with activists who raised the critique of male behavior as a powerful justification for expanding women's rights. Nevertheless, the tension between the goals of the traditional moralists and the feminist advocates for political rights had splintered pre–Civil War organizations. That the WCTU avoided that fate was due to the emergence of the one of the most extraordinary reform leaders in American history.[2]

In 1879, Frances Willard, a former dean of women and professor at Northwestern University in Illinois, became WCTU president and held the office until her death in 1898. Willard steered the organization toward political activism on behalf of social reforms that complemented the temperance drive for a renewed America. Willard's "Do Everything" exhortation became the WCTU motto. The president understood that her own devotion to activism could alienate conservative members, but skillfully justified progressive programs as weapons to achieve victory over alcohol. An early supporter of women's suffrage, Willard insisted that giving women voting rights aided the traditional female cause of "home protection." Beyond her gift for slogans, Willard had a commanding presence that elevated her into a revered figure within the WCTU. Through her tours of the South, traditionally inhospitable to social reformers, "Mother Willard" bolstered state unions. Urban southerners treated her "Do Everything" mission as consistent with the modernization and development of the region.[3]

In 1866 the Indiana Meeting of the Religious Society of Friends (Quakers), with the support of the Freedmen's Bureau, established Southland College near Helena, Arkansas, to offer education for African Americans. The Quaker leadership, shaped by nineteenth-century revivalism, also believed that the college could ignite a temperance wildfire that would free the Arkansas Delta "from the blighting and demoralizing effects of the greatest sin now existing in our country." Lydia Chase accompanied her husband, Amasa, to Southland after having participated in early women's demonstrations against Ohio saloons. In 1876, her temperance lecture at the Presbyterian church in Monticello moved the assembled women, several of whom had never seen a woman behind a pulpit, to organize the first local WCTU chapter in Arkansas. Women in other communities soon began to pin to their clothing the white ribbon, the WCTU badge.[4]

In 1879, the Forrest City union urged WCTU members to gather in June at Searcy to learn about the work of the various unions and to engage in a "frank interchange of sentiment." Meeting in a Searcy Baptist church, the delegates elected Annie T. Jones as president of the new Arkansas WCTU. A graduate of an elite Memphis academy, Jones was married to a prosperous businessman in the small Little Red River port town of West Point. The official history of the WCTU characterized her as "a very brilliant and aggressive woman for her time." The combination of education, social prominence, and confidence in the necessity for reform was representative of the organization's leaders. The WCTU conclave coincided with the convention of the recently organized, male-only state Christian Temperance Union. When the men's organization convened in the state Capitol building the following January, it agreed to seat "all persons ... who are known to be in sympathy with the temperance cause." Lydia Chase attended the convention and invited subscriptions to a temperance journal. The WCTU retained its separate identity, although apparently scheduling its state convention for the next several years to meet in conjunction with the Christian Temperance Union.[5]

Frances Willard's address in 1881 to the state WCTU meeting stimulated membership drives while her 1882 speech before the Arkansas state legislature underscored the organization's expanding influence. In 1888, seventy-five local unions, in addition to thirty-seven children's Loyal Temperance Legions (LTL), were identified at the state convention, which accepted reports from the volunteer heads or superintendents of the formal departments: Social Purity, Sabbath School, Sabbath Observance, Narcotics, Scientific Temperance Instruction, Influencing

Frances Willard, leader of the national WCTU, promoted the growth of the Arkansas union.

COURTESY OF OLD STATE HOUSE MUSEUM.

the Press, Juvenile Work, Evangelistic, Prison and Jail, Legislative, Temperance Literature, Heredity and Hygiene, Flower Mission, Impure Literature Suppression, Work among the Colored People, Use of Unfermented Wine, and Franchise. Boys and girls enrolled in a local LTL took the adult pledge to "abstain from intoxicating liquors" and sported brightly colored "Soldiers of Honor" ribbons. In 1889 a Batesville union member wrote that a young LTL girl refused to take an offered sip of whiskey while a physician closed a large wound in her skull: "I'm temperance; wouldn't take it, to save me."[6]

WCTU members, however, wanted the schools to reinforce the lessons children learned in LTL meetings. By 1882, the national WCTU demanded that states adopt "scientific temperance education" laws that required teachers to use health lessons to demonstrate the benefits of abstinence. Lawmakers in state after state readily approved these popular acts that pleased antialcohol activists but did not anger those opposed to restrictions on liquor sales. In 1899 the Arkansas General Assembly voted overwhelmingly for the Hillhouse Act, which planted temperance instruction into the classroom. Arkansas was one of the last states to take this step. Nevertheless, the long effort marked an early, sustained lobbying effort carried out by women.[7]

The Arkansas WCTU promoted temperance among black residents but was not among the eight southern states that established statewide African American unions, organizations often designated as "State WCTU No. 2." In Tennessee, for example, the growing number of African American unions emerged from the critical institutions of church and colleges. In contrast, Arkansas's "work among the colored people" was more in line with missionary paternalism than organization building, and between 1901 and 1911 no reports from this department were delivered at the Arkansas WCTU state conventions. The meeting records of 1916 reveal the first identification of local African-American unions, including organizations located in the east Arkansas communities of Grady, DeVall's Bluff, and Marianna. Unions in Winchester and in Tillar, where Sophronia Brown and Elana McGowan eventually secured 110 pledges of abstinence, stood out as the most active among the black chapters. Although middle-class African American women nurtured the growth of club federations in Little Rock and Pine Bluff, WCTU files do not indicate that they formed unions in these larger towns. The African American unions established before World War I disappeared from the 1920s WCTU rolls.[8]

The consensus among white WCTU members to accept the boundaries of segregation broke down over the question of the suffrage, or voting rights for women. Early suffrage leaders such as Clara McDiarmid, the founder of the Arkansas Equal Suffrage Association, were steadfast white-ribboners as well. First published in 1888, the *Woman's Chronicle* of Little Rock served as the official journal for both the suffrage association and the state WCTU. Annie T. Jones echoed the national "home protection" program when she declared in 1889 that permitting women to vote was "the only means to further the temperance movement and protect the youth of the country." The first WCTU president was emphasizing the conservative goals of suffrage to soothe hard feelings from the May 1888 state convention. The yellow ribbons worn by suffrage supporters blossomed at that meeting, and the majority of the delegates resolved that women should be given the ballot in municipal elections. Several local chapters objected strenuously. In February 1889, Susan B. Anthony delivered an address in Little Rock on the topic of "Woman and Temperance." Lydia Chase, in her WCTU column published in the *Woman's Chronicle,* urged her members to "hear this gifted woman, though they may differ from her on the question which she has espoused as her life's work—Woman's Suffrage."[9]

Although deprived of the vote, women in Arkansas had other means to beard "king alcohol." In 1871, the Republican Reconstruction legislature permitted the majority of the voters within a town to petition for the removal of retail liquor outlets within three miles of an academy or a college. Four years later a similar law was approved with a significant revision: the petition to halt alcohol sales within three miles of an educational institution had to be signed by the majority of adult residents. In effect, the measure enabled women to exercise political power, a breakthrough confirmed in subsequent legislation. In 1880 the state Supreme Court ruled that allowing female petitioners to close down saloons did not contradict election law: "There is no good reason why women and girls, if adults, should not join in such petitions. They are as deeply interested in removing temptations to dissipation and vice from pupils of schools, and preserving good morals in communities where such institutions of learning are located, as men are." In 1889, six Yell County women traveled twenty rugged miles to Danville to present to the county court petitions that would end alcohol sales in their hometown of Dardanelle. They were forced to attend court sessions each day for a week and a half and fend off challenges from "the liquor men" as to the authenticity of the signatures. After the temperance women patiently vouched for each name, the county officials accepted the petitions. One of the petitioners observed that the opponents were "the worst whipped set of men" ever to be seen.[10]

Soon an 1879 local option law, rather than the three-mile act, became the primary engine for piecemeal prohibition. The statute required voters within a township or incorporated town to vote every two years on whether or not to permit the granting of licenses to sell alcohol in quantities of less than five gallons. If the license option failed to gain a majority, then saloons were out of business for at least two years. More often than not, a vote against liquor in one election kept the locality permanently dry. Despite their exclusion from the voting booth, some WCTU members transformed the old techniques of moral persuasion into political activism. An 1888 notice in the *Woman's Chronicle* reported that efforts to influence men to vote against licensing included "the presence of quite a number of ladies at the polls in Little Rock." The capital city's bars remained opened, but one woman buttonholing voters during the same election helped move Baxter County to the dry column for the first time.[11]

Local law officers were obligated to launch forays against moonshiners and bootleggers when communities banned alcoholic drink sales. In 1911, Sid McMath, the Columbia County sheriff and grandfather of a future governor, was ambushed and killed as he approached a moonshine hideout in an abandoned sawmill. In June 1915 a raid on an illegal saloon by an Arkansas posse on Island 37 in the Mississippi River led to the shooting death of the Mississippi County sheriff. The blind tiger's owner, who was not present during the shootout, was taken from the Osceola jail and lynched by the lawman's constituents. Yet, the antialcohol organizations held both apathetic constables and vexing legal exceptions responsible for blatant evasions of local option regulations. A druggist could sell alcohol to a customer presenting a doctor's prescription that cited a medical need. Not surprisingly, the health of many Arkansans went into immediate decline. In February 1880 a letter writer to the Magnolia newspaper observed, "Is it against the law to sell alcoholic or vinous liquors, except for medicinal purposes? If it is, I think three-fourths of the men in the county are under medical treatment."

Dramatization of wife compelling husband to sign an abstinence pledge.

LIBRARY OF CONGRESS, PRINTS AND PHOTOGRAPHS DIVISION.

In 1896 a Texarkana pharmacist employed a physician to do nothing but write prescriptions for alcohol.[12]

Dissatisfaction with enforcement measures and the slow trickle of localities voting out saloons throughout the 1880s stoked support for statewide prohibition in some temperance circles. In 1884, the state convention of the men's temperance organization adopted a resolution that its members should support only political candidates committed to prohibition. Both within the convention and throughout the antiliquor ranks, this position stirred strong passions and disagreements. This new political stance challenged Democratic dominance in the state as insurgent agrarian organizations and the national Prohibition party began to offer dry advocates electoral alternatives. In 1886 members of the Agricultural Wheel, an organization founded to defend the interests of small farmers, convened to nominate a slate of candidates to vie against the Democrats and offer a party platform with a prohibition plank. Two years later, delegates from seventeen counties met in Little Rock to form an Arkansas affiliate of the Prohibition party, which favored a national constitutional amendment to ban all alcohol and backed women's voting rights.[13]

Those WCTU leaders in Arkansas who also favored suffrage welcomed the new political organizations, which viewed women as notable allies in their battles against the established parties. The editor of the *Woman's Chronicle* praised the Agricultural Wheel for admitting women as delegates to its 1888 nominating convention: "All honor to the Wheel! We bid you God speed, our sisters." By this year, Frances Willard had aligned the national WCTU with the Prohibition party. In Arkansas, Bernie Babcock, the noted suffragist and prohibitionist repeatedly denounced both Democrats and Republicans as minions of John Barleycorn: "But in the sunset of the nineteenth century a party has arisen in its manhood and power that recognizes the injustice done the women of our land; that recognizes the fact that our law-abiding, peace-loving mother should have the right to make the laws by which herself and her children are governed as well as has her party-loving, law-breaking husband. . . . To this party do broken-hearted women look for succor, and through this party will come the woman's liberty."[14]

Nevertheless, the Prohibition party attracted few votes in Arkansas for either its presidential nominees or its state candidates. Recognizing the unlikelihood of gaining state office, the party in 1896 gave serious consideration to nominating a woman for governor. While it did not take this step, the state Prohibition party consistently included women in its delegation to the national convention. In 1906, Silas C. Swallow secured 992 votes, registering the best showing in Arkansas by a Prohibition party presidential nominee. Temperance discontent with the Democratic party peaked that election year as party primary voters chose Gov. Jeff Davis for a U.S. Senate seat. Exploiting rural resentment of urban business interests, Davis had served three terms as governor despite accusations from opponents that he masked his heavy drinking by guzzling "Wizard Oil," a patent medicine that purported to restore sobriety quickly. In May 1902, Davis was expelled from the Second Baptist Church in Little Rock on charges of public drunkenness and gambling. The moralists' disapproval bolstered Davis's claims that he was persecuted by the well-born and the town elites, and his supporters roared when he admitted that he was only a "pint Baptist" compared to the "quart Baptists" arrayed against him. Throughout his last two gubernatorial terms, Davis vetoed temperance bills and pardoned hundreds of operators of blind tigers. In Little Rock on February 15, 1906, Carry Nation, the nation's most famous antialcohol activist, excoriated Davis as "the worst governor in the Union."[15]

In 1900, Nation had begun attacking Kansas saloons, first with a mallet and then with a hatchet. Her speaking tours throughout the United States, as well as in Scotland and England, enhanced her fame and notoriety. Children invented games in which boys would build "saloon forts" and girls would launch assaults with sticks and stones. The national WCTU, however, viewed her as overly controversial and disavowed her tactics. The day after her condemnation of Davis, Nation was arrested in Hot Springs when she entered a Central Avenue bar and remonstrated the patrons. Nevertheless, Nation's expeditions into Arkansas won her admirers, and she had high regard for the state. In 1908 she purchased a farm and cabin outside of Eureka Springs as a retirement haven: "The water is the purest, the scenery is not surpassed,

Gov. Jeff Davis rebuffed attacks by temperance leaders.

and the mountain air is life-giving. . . . I believe the mountains of the Ozarks to be the future health resorts of this country." The following year she moved into a large house on Steele Street in Eureka Springs. Christened "Hatchet Hall," the house became a rescue mission for battered women, a school, and a rest home for the elderly. In January 1911, Carry Nation collapsed while addressing a Eureka Springs audience, reportedly muttering before she fell, "I have done what I could." She remained bedridden until dying six months later.[16]

Carry Nation's blast against Gov. Davis in 1906 had been unleashed at the state meeting of the Anti-Saloon League (ASL). She had forced her way without invitation into the convention of a dry organization that did not share her contempt for the Democratic party nor her fervor for a general state prohibition law. In 1893, Howard Russell had organized the Ohio Anti-Saloon League, which two years later became the basis for a national organization. The creation of the Anti-Saloon League reflected disapproval of both the broad social reform program of the WCTU and the union's alliance with the Prohibition party. In 1894 male delegates met in Little Rock to form the "No License Association," the forerunner of the state ASL. The group determined to achieve prohibition incrementally through local option election victories and through pressure on legislators to close loopholes in current statutes. This lobbying strategy required cooperation with powerful Democratic officeholders and dismissed women's suffrage as a distraction. The president of the new association was George F. Thornburgh, a former speaker of the state House of Representatives, who would become the dominant figure in the antialcohol movement in the early twentieth century.[17]

In contrast to the antebellum societies, the ASL concerned itself less with the drinker than with the saloon as the source of social turmoil and political corruption. Changes in drinking patterns seemed to justify the cautionary tales in temperance writings. In the late nineteenth century, Americans increasingly spurned whiskey in favor of beer, and the lack of home refrigeration required imbibers to seek out draft lager at the corner tavern. In addition, the fierce competition among beer manufacturers led brewers to acquire or set up their own saloons, the number of which doubled in the United States between 1880 and 1900.

Carry Nation retired to Arkansas following a decade of attacking saloons.

Brewers pressured barkeeps to keep their businesses open past legal closing times, to entice drinkers with gambling and bawdy vaudeville style
acts, and to never, ever tell a customer that he has had enough. In 1890
the *Woman's Chronicle* lamented a newly opened "place of amusement"
near the state Capitol building: "Reports come to us of mothers lament-
ing that their boys are allured there to spend hours in witnessing degrad-
ing exhibitions, and between the acts, men standing fair in the
community, set the example of drinking with women they would shrink
from recognizing as associates. . . ." In 1912, the state's Methodist newspaper laid out the case against saloons: "The saloons of Little Rock made
policemen, the hired protectors of the people, so drunk that ten had to
be discharged. There are more oaths and obscene language in the saloons
than in all other places. Most of the fights and brawls occur in or near
the saloons."[18]

Those drinking emporiums catering to prosperous customers provided less fodder for temperance propaganda. Beginning in the 1870s,
brothers Angelo and John Marre operated on Markham Street in Little
Rock the Senate Saloon and Billiard Parlor, one of the first of the city's
saloons to boast electric lights. Plaster figures of Rip Van Winkle perched
atop the walnut bar, which was guarded on either end by alabaster lions.
Ceiling frescoes depicted bacchanalian romps. An archway and all the
windows were fitted with Venetian glass. The Marres understood the
advantage of their high-toned address. They ordered a shipment of the
same marble found in the elegant lobby of the Capital Hotel across the
street. Nevertheless, the refined atmosphere of some saloons did not
deter prohibitionists from calling to task pillars of the community. In a
1908 speech, W. E. Atkinson, editor of the state *Baptist Advance,* insisted
that the liquor trade was propped up with the connivance of attorneys,
physicians, and other professionals. Respectable surroundings could not
efface the presence of king alcohol: "You walk into a place of business
and smell whisky on the breath of the man who waits upon you."[19]

In 1899 the No License Association evolved into the state Anti-
Saloon League affiliate, with Atkinson as the first president. The state
organization wished to follow the example of the national ASL, which
took up the pressure politics pioneered by the WCTU. By 1906, over
half of the counties and 60 percent of the towns in the United States

The elaborate bar at Angelo Marre's saloon attracted an elite Little Rock clientele.

COURTESY OF ARKANSAS HISTORY COMMISSION.

had banned saloons. Arkansas marched with the rest of the nation; that year 54 of the 75 counties voted dry in the required biannual local option elections. In that same year, however, contention between Protestant denominational leaders split the male temperance ranks into rival factions.[20]

Believing the ASL chapter ineffective, George Thornburgh, a prominent Methodist, instigated the schism that led to the formation

of the Inter-Church Temperance Federation. Governed by Methodist
and Presbyterian ministers, the federation adopted its constitution the
day before Carry Nation barged into what was then a smaller, Baptist-
dominated ASL convention. From 1906 through the fall of 1907,
Atkinson charged in the *Baptist Advance* that the Rev. Edward A. Tabor,
the superintendent of the upstart group, was soliciting donations and
support at the expense of the existing ASL. Barbed accusations flew
across the sectarian lines. Tabor compared Atkinson's recalcitrance to
that of the pagans in ancient Ephesus who rebuffed the Apostle Paul,
while Atkinson denied that his Baptist church shared a common lineage
with Methodism and Presbyterianism, which he characterized as "daughters of an old whore" (presumably the Roman Catholic church). In 1907,
Thornburgh's federation triumphed when the national ASL office recognized it as the official state chapter. Two years later, however, Tabor's
Baptist critics gained some satisfaction when the superintendent of the
newly sanctioned Arkansas ASL resigned following revelations of his
whiskey drinking. The state ASL "secret service," set up to identify blind
tigers, found a bottle in Tabor's satchel.[21]

In 1910, Thornburgh announced the ASL was discarding its local
option strategy in favor of a campaign for statewide prohibition. In 1912
he also departed from the ASL practice of not backing candidates when
he endorsed the reelection of Gov. George Donaghey, who was challenged by U.S. Rep. Joseph T. Robinson. Donaghey favored state prohibition while Robinson preferred the continuation of the local option
system. Robinson's victory in the March Democratic primary left
Donaghey time to stump for the initiated prohibition act drafted by the
ASL. Its fate was to be decided in the state's general election in September.
The strong majorities against saloons in the local option elections fed
the optimism of ASL leaders, who were also buoyed by favorable resolutions in recent Democratic party state conventions. Still, Thornburgh's
quest for prohibition through popular referendum was a miscalculation.[22]

Robinson's aversion to prohibition indicated the political establishment was not of one mind on the issue. The opposition to the act by
powerful office holders was buttressed by interest groups funded by liquor
retailers and business development interests. One of Robinson's advisers

reminded him that candidates for governor had little chance without the blessings of the "whiskey ring." On the other side, Thornburgh and the ASL could not mobilize a united temperance army. Not surprisingly, the *Baptist Advance* questioned the Methodist leader's strategy. The WCTU leadership also insisted that prohibition was certain to come up short in a popular vote and charged that "the State Anti-Saloon League did not know what it is doing, that it had lost its moorings and that whiskey people were using it as a leverage." These critics of Thornburgh insisted that manipulation of the election process by county machines doomed any chance for gaining a dry law by referendum. By June 1912, the ASL was ready to throw in the towel but soldiered on when it failed to expunge the proposed act from the ballot. In the end, the WCTU reluctantly urged its members to work on behalf of the measure. Following the decisive defeat of the proposal, Thornburgh claimed his cause was swamped by entrenched interests and underhanded methods: "We had not the money to compete with the unlimited advertising fund of the liquor forces, we would not follow them in their outrageous mis-representations, and we could not as honorable men trade with the negroes for their votes." Lula Markwell, president of the WCTU, echoed these points, insisting "that negroes have ruled at the ballot box" through the dereliction of "white Christians." The paternalism of white antiliquor forces festered into overt racism when African Americans declined to support a temperance measure.[23]

Prohibitionists charged that their liquor rivals were behind the successful drive to include on the September 1912 ballot a "grandfather clause" amendment to the constitution that would have effectively ended African American voting in Arkansas. In 1906, Jeff Davis had compelled the Democratic party to adopt the whites-only restriction in primary contests, but procedures excluding blacks from the polls during general elections were less sweeping. The fears of the ASL and the WCTU that the inclusion of the grandfather clause would spur a turnout of antipro-hibitionist voters were confirmed when both initiated acts were soundly beaten in counties with significant African American populations. Even though the temperance groups took no position on the failed disfran-chisement proposal, Gov. Donaghey had coupled his public efforts on behalf of prohibition with energetic advocacy for disfranchisement.[24]

Prohibitionists turned from ballot proposals to the Arkansas legislature. The first victory for the dry lobby was an overhaul of the 1870s local option regulations. Turmoil surrounded the biannual liquor license elections, and the flagrant vote tampering troubled political bosses, who feared giving reformers ammunition. In state senator L. Clyde Going's northeast Arkansas district, white and black millworkers labored long hours manufacturing lumber products and intermingled during their free time in nearby saloons. A local prohibition movement failed to

Gov. George Donaghey believed that liquor interests were a source of political corruption.

Courtesy of Arkansas History Commission.

eradicate these rowdy establishments, which mocked piety and segregation. In 1913 Going secured legislative approval for a bill that tacked on a new requirement before saloons in incorporated towns could open for business. In those localities voting wet, officials were still unable to grant licenses until presented with a petition supporting liquor sales that was signed by the majority of *adult white residents*. Removing African Americans and including white women in the local option system fit with the strategy to create rock-solid majorities for prohibition. In 1914, the state attorney general issued an opinion that the Going law's exclusion of black petitioners violated the equal privileges and immunities clause in the Fourteenth Amendment to the U.S. Constitution, a position upheld by a circuit court decision that struck down the law as unconstitutional. In April, however, the state Supreme Court overruled that finding on the grounds that the regulation of liquor was a legitimate exercise of the state's police powers and that such authority was not constrained by constitutional protections of citizens' rights.[25]

By the end of 1914, only nine counties had overcome the legal hurdles to keep their bars open. Even so, the prohibitionists denounced the sprouting of saloons in unincorporated villages in otherwise dry counties. Thornburgh and others declared that only statewide prohibition could close this loophole in the Going law. With the vast majority of lawmakers in the 1915 session hailing from dry counties, the opposition had little chance to kill the Newberry bill that banned the manufacture, sale, and giving away of alcohol in Arkansas. Senator Clyde Going attempted to sidetrack the bill with an amendment to submit prohibition to popular vote but surrendered to the inevitable. Gov. George W. Hays had also favored holding a referendum on the issue but changed course after Thornburgh and other dry leaders paid a visit. On February 6, 1915, the governor signed the measure. About forty-five minutes before Hays affixed his signature, fifty-three Little Rock liquor dealers applied for and were granted licenses although some hopefuls in line failed to secure authorization before the county clerk received the telephone call from the governor's office. Proprietors holding licenses before enactment of the bill could remain in business until January 1, 1916. In contrast to earlier liquor regulations, the law included no exceptions for medical prescriptions or for the preservation of the native wine industry.[26]

Liquor business associations and sympathetic wets tested their belief in the wisdom of the people by campaigning for an initiated act to repeal the Newberry measure in favor of reestablishing the local option process. In the 1916 general election, the proposal met defeat by an almost two-to-one margin. In organizing their forces, the white prohibitionists took a lesson from the 1912 election and sought the public endorsement of prominent African American leaders including Scipio Jones,

Gov. Charles Brough was both a supporter of women's suffrage and prohibition.

Courtesy of Butler Center of Arkansas Studies, Central Arkansas Library System.

the legendary attorney; Bishop James M. Conner, leader of the state AME conference; and the Rev. Joseph A. Booker, president of Arkansas Baptist College. This was also the year that the WCTU first recognized local black unions, and the temperance women once again rallied to shape a political issue through grassroots activism. Minnie Rutherford Fuller, WCTU president, reported that "the women of our loyal band toiled early and late, met one another on the highways coming from different directions, scattering leaflets and pasting posters, telling our voters, in no uncertain terms, the importance of voting against Act No. 2."[27]

In 1917, Arkansas became one of the first states to enact a "bone-dry" law when the legislature banned the shipment of liquor into the state. Gov. Charles Brough signed the measure before addressing a meeting of the state chamber of commerce at the Marion Hotel, a long-time favorite haunt of legislators who sealed deals over glasses of bourbon. The assembled businessmen serenaded Brough with "How Dry I Am." American entry into World War I that year provided the final impetus for the national Prohibition movement to unfurl a victory banner. Moved by demands that grain stocks must be reserved for food and by denouncements of German brewers, Congress submitted the dry amendment to the states. In January 1919, Arkansas became the 27th state to ratify the Eighteenth Amendment, an anticlimax to a battle already won.[28]

Nineteenth–Century Saloons

Although grocery stores sold liquor, most nineteenth–century urban drinkers frequented saloons. Proprietors eagerly served thirsty customers, and the resulting public drunkenness and brawling stoked the fervor of prohibitionists.

Saloons drew loyal male customers defiant of public disapproval.

A Newark, Independence County saloon, circa 1900.

A Faulkner County saloon, circa 1920.

Cleaning Up Smackover

Smackover barrelhouse or saloon constructed from oil barrels and sawed timber.

In November 1922, armed hooded figures attacked illegal saloons and gambling houses that had flourished outside of Smackover (Union County) after the oil boom.

*Armed citizens prepared
to maintain order.*

*A destroyed gambling den
after the vigilante attack.*

The Dry Kingdom
Under Assault

4

They hired men with the holly club
To flay him skin from bone
And the miller he served him worse than that
For he ground him between two stones
Here's Little Sir John in a nut brown bowl

NONE OF THE RESOLUTIONS presented at the 1919 state WCTU convention addressed the problem of alcohol. The union supported the League of Nations and restrictions on tobacco as well as warning about the influence of movies: "Whereas, the uncensored motion picture show has become such a menace to the morals of our girls and boys. Resolved, that the WCTU endorse the censorship of motion pictures and throw all their splendid energies into getting a bill through our next legislature." During the 1920s members at annual meetings learned from the Department of Americanization that immigrants were ignorant of temperance principles and from the Department of Bible in Public Schools that laws were needed to ensure scripture recitation in the classroom. The emphasis upon moral reform reflected the concerns and outlook of Lula Markwell, a former WCTU president. Markwell later served as head of the Little Rock Board for Censorship of Amusements. By contrast, Minnie Rutherford Fuller, president of the Union when Prohibition was achieved, had promoted social welfare and political rights in the years leading up to World War I. She organized an early suffrage group, drafted the 1911 law establishing juvenile courts, and in 1914 compiled a digest of laws governing women and children that justified expansion of married women's property and legal rights. Fuller once observed that she was performing "the sentinel duty of the lobbyist." Nevertheless, the addition of Prohibition and women's voting rights to the U.S. constitution shifted the union members from crusaders to defenders of the new status quo.[1]

Beyond education and propaganda, preserving Prohibition also required enforcement of laws. Before 1920 the ASL had employed detectives and designated squads of members to uncover illegal liquor operations. National Prohibition, however, had the potential to make private policing actions unnecessary. In the past, federal agents had been primarily concerned with catching moonshiners for making untaxed liquor, while local officers in dry counties wanted to round up those who sold drinks without a license. General Prohibition laws abolished all the jurisdictional contradictions as the rising numbers of illegal liquor sellers spurred popular demands for stern action. Ernest Pyle, the south Arkansas wildcatter, recalled that by the mid-1920s "both Columbia and Union counties were doing everything in their power to stop moonshining and bootlegging. When they went out after somebody, if they broke and ran, they would shoot them." The crackdown reflected the uncompromising policies of Gov. Tom J. Terral, whose 1924 election was aided by his membership in the era's most active prohibitionist organization, the Ku Klux Klan.[2]

Beginning in the summer of 1921, Klan organizers radiated from Little Rock to form klaverns, or local chapters, throughout the state. Eventually, the organization claimed around fifty thousand members in Arkansas. The preponderance of Klan members shared the social and economic backgrounds of old-line temperance organizers. Klaverns were usually based in towns and enrolled white, middle-class men who believed in taking action to restore the moral and religious order of the community. While the Klan was a male order, the Women of the Ku Klux Klan, a sanctioned auxiliary, was founded and headquartered in Little Rock. Lula Markwell, the former WCTU president, was the first Imperial Commander. Shortly after the organization's founding in 1923, Markwell embarked on a recruiting swing of western states, and within a few months the Women of the Klan claimed 250,000 members in thirty-six states. In 1924 Markwell resigned, following bitter disputes with James Comer, the Arkansas Grand Dragon, who treated the Women of the Klan as part of his nascent political machine. Comer installed his girlfriend and future wife as the new Imperial Commander.[3]

The state's small immigrant population and oppressive segregation system reduced the Klan's opportunities to carry out its nativist and racist program in Arkansas. In contrast, bootleggers and moonshiners were flouting the law and community morals. The oil boom in Union County sparked the proliferation of lucrative gambling dens, brothels, and barrel houses (saloons), which, in turn, boosted the local Ku Klux Klan rolls. In November 1922, two hundred hooded men, describing

A 1920s Ku Klux Klan gathering in Union County.

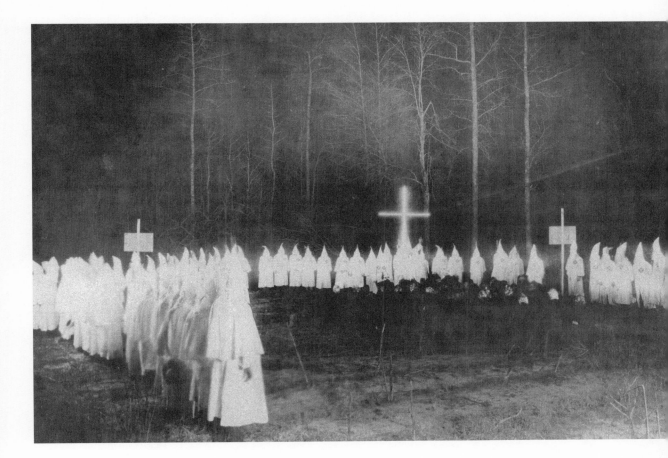

themselves as the "Cleanup Committee," invaded the "Shotgun Valley" and "Pistol Hill" districts near Smackover, torching buildings and killing one man when they met with scattered armed resistance. The Ouachita County sheriff estimated that the Klan riot expelled around two thousand individuals associated with the vice trade.[4]

More commonly, mass vigilante actions were unnecessary since Klan members for a time controlled city and county governments throughout the state. In Monticello, where the mayor and half the city aldermen belonged to the Klan, the "Shock Committee" of Klan No. 108 aided sympathetic law enforcement officers by offering rewards to those identifying Prohibition violators. Klansmen caught drinking were booted from the chapter, the same treatment afforded backsliders by early temperance societies. In August 1925, the Rev. Harry G. Knowles, a popular Klan lecturer, accompanied Little Rock detectives in the arrest of a bootlegger after the clergyman's son and another officer purchased whiskey to gain evidence against the culprit. Later that month, Homer Adkins, who had been elected Pulaski County sheriff as part of a Klan slate, and two deputies raided a private home near Wrightsville and arrested twelve African Americans and two whites. The residence served as well-known saloon in which "liquor was being served on two large tables, equipped with bells to ring for service." Adkins characterized the arrests as part of a concentrated campaign that had over the course of the previous weeks led to the seizure of one thousand bottles of whiskey. The contents were emptied into the Arkansas River. Nearly all of those taken into custody in these Adkins's raids were African American.[5]

The 1925 implosion of the Arkansas Klan amid charges of corruption and political arrogance occurred as the national Ku Klux Klan was dissolving. The moralist campaigns against modernity in the United States were flagging by the end of the decade. Prominent conservative business leaders funded and supported anti-Prohibition organizations on the grounds that the "noble experiment" had dangerously expanded federal authority, outlawed an entire industry without compensation, and undermined respect for the law through lax enforcement of the Volstead Act (the national Prohibition statute). Formed in 1929, the Women's Organization for National Prohibition Reform became the largest group mobilized to repeal the Eighteenth Amendment and soon boasted more members than the WCTU. Only Arkansas and five other states lacked chapters of this newest women's political organization. Yet, even stalwart Arkansas was wavering.[6]

In 1928 the Democratic party nominated Al Smith, the anti-prohibitionist governor of New York, for the presidency and Senator Joseph T. Robinson from Arkansas as his running mate. The militant

Sheriff Homer Adkins made headlines with his raids against Pulaski County speakeasies and was later elected governor.

COURTESY OF OLD STATE HOUSE MUSEUM.

dry forces in the state called the ticket a betrayal and veered toward a collision with the state's political establishment. Alexander Copeland Millar, a Methodist clergymen and ASL president, openly led a dissident group of anti-Smith Democrats and urged the election of the Republican presidential candidate, Herbert Hoover. The WCTU executives were more disingenuous. In September 1928, President Jeannie Carr Pittman was compelled by discontent within local unions to issue a statement: "There seems to be a rumor afloat that the President has pledged the state W.C.T.U. to Republicanism. She pleads 'not guilty' to the charge." Pittman offered a convoluted interpretation of the national WCTU mandate to support a dry candidate to mean "not going into Republicanism or Democracy as such, but being big enough and fine enough to stand by the purpose for which we came into being." Chided by allies such as the editors of the *Arkansas Gazette* and unable to deliver their own members, the Prohibition groups failed to dislodge Arkansas from the Democratic column in the November election.[7]

As the Great Depression spread, President Hoover's adamant loyalty to Prohibition only deepened his unpopularity. During the 1932 campaign, the Democratic party's endorsement of repeal more clearly distinguished it from the rival GOP than Franklin D. Roosevelt's economic proposals, which were vague and conventional. The Democratic landslide emboldened the new U.S. Senate majority leader, Joseph T. Robinson, to pressure his colleagues into approving the resolution for a constitutional amendment to repeal the Eighteenth. In accordance with the resolution, states were to conduct elections for delegates who would meet in conventions to determine whether or not to ratify the proposed amendment. The Arkansas General Assembly made the procedure more democratic by holding a referendum on repeal of Prohibition along with the election of convention members in each county. Delegates were required to rubber-stamp the outcome of the referendum. The July 18, 1933, election date made Arkansas one of the first southern states to consider the amendment, and repeal proponents understood that a favorable outcome in this bulwark of temperance foreshadowed adoption of the Twenty-first Amendment.[8]

During the summer, the Roosevelt Repeal Club and the United Prohibition forces fought their battle through community rallies, caravans of volunteer speakers, pamphlets, and debates on radio. The refer-endum results were decisive: 67,622 voted for repeal as opposed to 46,091 against, with 52 of the 75 counties favoring Prohibition's demise. On August 1 the convention officially ratified the repeal amendment. Much like the temperance pioneers before the Civil War, the latter-day advocates blamed the lukewarm faithful rather than give credit to the armies of darkness. In September 1933, Cora Gillespie, president of the WCTU, confessed, "Our response to the wet vote in Arkansas is inex-pressible sorrow. . . . The line broke because the church members did not stand for the law."[9]

Senator Joseph T. Robinson never embraced the prohibition movement and moved quickly to draft a repeal amendment to the Constitution.

COURTESY OF OLD STATE HOUSE MUSEUM.

Prohibition Era in Arkansas

The majority of Arkansans welcomed the coming of national Prohibition in the 1920s, but many residents proved creative in finding ways to drink. Widespread violations of the law led to growing weariness with the "noble experiment" and its most prominent advocate, President Herbert Hoover.

Prohibition laws allowed distribution of commercial grain alcohol, which was often used to produce illegal liquor.

Specially designed flasks were carried discreetly in this businessman's case.

Courtesy of Old State House Museum.

Cigar flasks easily fitted into a suit pocket.

Courtesy of Old State House Museum.

Both the 1930s economic collapse and unpopularity of Prohibition made President Herbert Hoover a frequent target of ridicule.

Cold War: Conflict and Coexistence

5

Here's Little Sir John in a nut brown bowl
And brandy in the glass
And Little Sir John in the nut brown bowl
Proved the stronger man at last
For the huntsman he can't hunt the fox
Nor so loudly blow his horn
And the tinker he can't mend kettle nor pot
Without a little of the Barleycorn.

ARKANSANS COULD TOAST Sir John's resurrection, but only with low-alcohol beer and wine. A few weeks after the ratification convention adjourned, the General Assembly, in a special session, legalized the manufacture and sale of beer and wine containing no more that 3.2 percent of alcohol by weight. The lawmakers imposed new taxes on liquor manufacturers and retailers. The special consideration for wine returned to the traditional protectionism of a distinctive industry.[1]

Arkansas had been a pioneer wine-producing state in the region. German-Swiss immigrants settling in Franklin County in the 1870s noted that the soil and climate of the Ozark foothills were well-suited for grape cultivation. Coal miners and railroad workers were the customers for early winemakers such as Johann Wiederkehr, Jacob Post, and Alfred Sax. The first wines were produced from native berries and grapes, but Joseph Bachman and other grape breeders soon developed cultivars that gained national recognition. In the early twentieth century the Italian immigrants who established Tontitown in Washington County found the soil suitable for growing Concord grapes, and several families established wineries, which soon gave way to more successful juice operations. During the Prohibition era, vintners had to market their wine grapes as suitable for eating. Upon repeal, winemaking struck some as a promising craft in the midst of a ruined economy, and they set up new operations in towns such as Monticello, Texarkana, Conway, and Little Rock. Eventually the federal government licensed 147 wineries although only about dozen had substantial production.[2]

Gov. Marion Futrell's policy of low taxes and reduced expenditures during the Depression was underwritten by the Federal Emergency Relief Administration (FERA), which absorbed almost all the welfare costs and kept the public schools open. By early 1935, Harry Hopkins, the FERA director, advised the governor that he would withhold federal dollars if the state did not begin to pay its fair share of relief and education costs. Facing this ultimatum, Futrell proposed that the legislature enact a variety of revenue measures, including the legalization and taxation of all alcoholic beverages. However, this most conservative of governors favored ensuring order through a government monopoly rather than simply regulating the peddlers of demon rum: "Any system of control which carries with it the possibility and hope of profit to individuals will never be successful. . . . The licensed dealers would be interested in making money and would be no better than the saloonist of old days . . . All sales should be made by the state." Futrell also regarded favorably an idea floated by a Fort Smith attorney to have the state enter into the production end of the market by setting up a whiskey distillery on the grounds of an abandoned state penitentiary. Free of federal taxation, the "convict corn" squeezings would undercut the bootleggers' prices, and the operation would keep prisoners busy during the winter when the crop fields were idled. The Fort Smith lawyer noted that expertise was not an issue; a fair number of convicts were already familiar with the distilling process.[3]

Although the General Assembly deferred to Futrell in approving most elements of his revenue program, the liquor retailers retained considerable influence, and the 1935 repeal of state prohibition laws revived the license system. Predictably, the legislative debate over the bill introduced by Harve B. Thorn, speaker of the house, turned not on who should sell liquor but whether it should be sold at all. The drys were undone by the strong consensus that Prohibition was a failed example of social engineering that had benefited primarily the bootleggers. Nevertheless, the vote on the repeal was close in both chambers. The Immanuel Baptist Church of Little Rock booted from its fellowship Vophie N. Carter, the representative from Pulaski County who cast a crucial aye vote in the House. Carter's outraged colleagues introduced a resolution testifying to his "integrity, honesty, sincerity, and Christianity," while the Columbia County representative told the churchless legislator that he would be welcomed by the Baptist congregation in Magnolia. Suspicious that the enforcement of the new liquor regulations could be watered down, Futrell waited until the General Assembly adjourned before signing the Thorn bill. The law did acknowledge the governor's objections to the revival of saloons by refusing to permit the sale of alcohol by the glass or individual drink.[4]

Upon the adoption of the repeal measure, all of Arkansas was wet and the prohibitionists could regain territory only through following a new local option procedure. Under the old system, elections on the question of liquor sales occurred automatically every two years. The 1935 act required the dry forces to submit a petition signed by 35 percent of the voters in a locality before officials could hold a special election on whether or not to halt alcohol sales. The law permitted no more than one such local referendum every three years. The signature requirement was a formidable barrier, and liquor remained available in sections of the state that had not permitted legal sales since the late nineteenth century. Throughout the 1930s the ASL attempted to revise the local option provision through a statewide initiated act and finally achieved success in 1942 by insisting that its proposal advanced good government and local democracy.[5]

The proposed act lowered the required proportion of signatures to 15 percent and voided limitations on the frequency of elections. Advocates of the change downplayed the possibility of closed retail package stores and emphasized that the constitution required local petitions

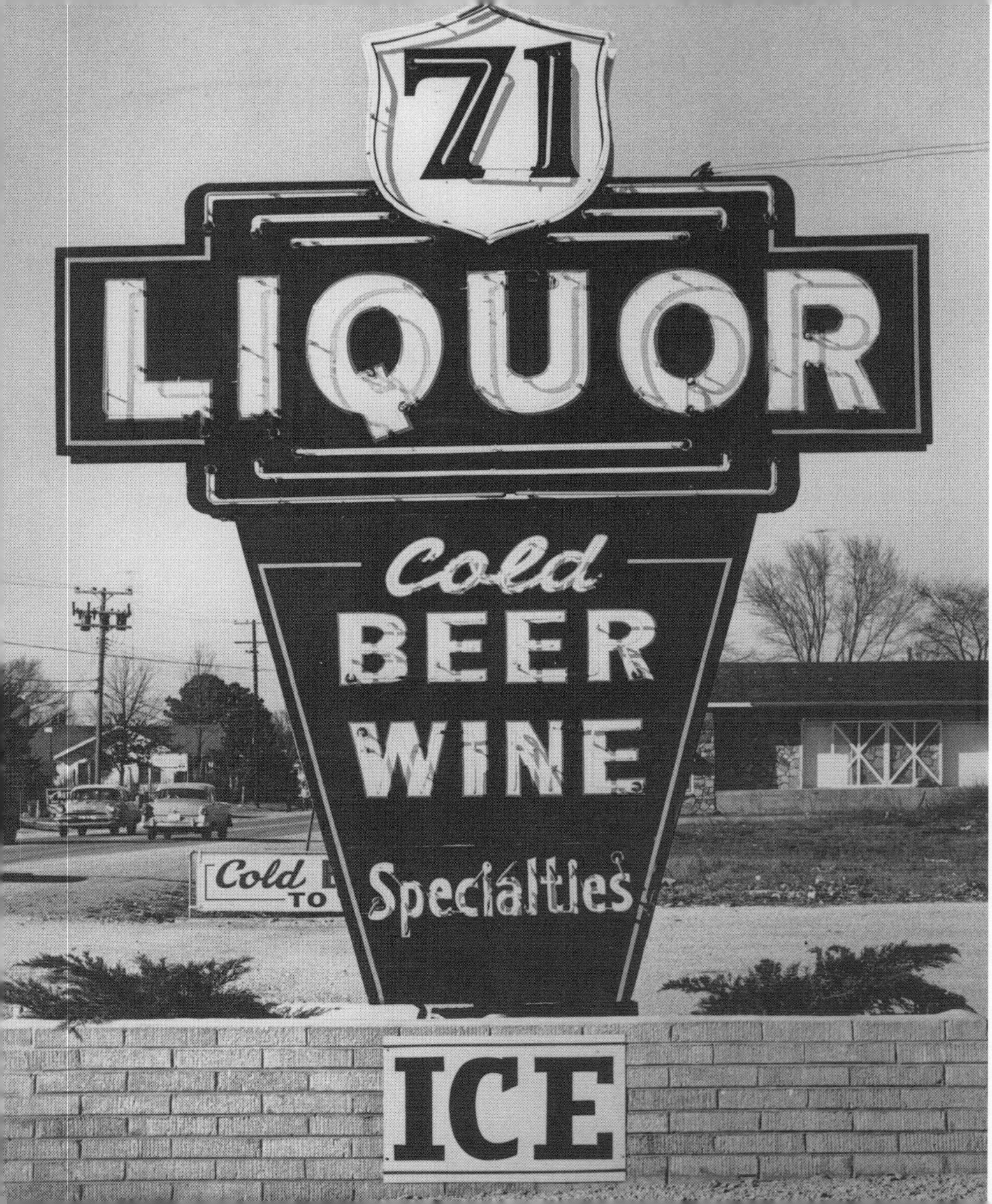
71
LIQUOR
Cold
BEER
WINE
Specialties
ICE
Cold
TO

on other issues to include only 15 percent of eligible signatures. A front page *Arkansas Gazette* editorial presented it as a matter of simple fairness: "Initiated Act No. 1 is not a prohibition law or a liquor law, but an election law to place the machinery for local option legislation on the same basis with other local initiated legislation." In November 1942 a sizable majority of voters handed the dry groups their first victory since Prohibition. Of course, the antiliquor activists had no intention of waiting on a homegrown, democratic groundswell to oust demon rum from towns and counties. In 1943 the drys won thirty-two of forty local option elections following coordinated petition drives by the state ASL and their Protestant allies.[6]

As had their pre-World War I counterparts, the post-World War II Arkansas prohibitionists believed that local triumphs built momentum for statewide abolition of liquor sales. At the national level, however, the antialcohol forces were falling away. After Pearl Harbor, they repeated to no avail the arguments raised during World War I that the nation should not waste grain on whiskey or expose soldiers to its poisonous effects. Consumption rose during World War II. In 1948 the ASL, smaller and organizationally infirm, changed its name to the Temperance League of America. The Arkansas chapter followed suit, and it was the Temperance League of Arkansas that launched the last prohibitionist crusade in the state. Clyde C. Coulter, executive director of the League, noted that the state would be the first to attempt to overturn legalization of alcohol since the approval of the Twenty-first amendment: "All over the nation wet and dry forces have been watching Arkansas for this action."[7]

The League drafted Initiated Act 2 of 1950 to repeal the 1935 liquor measure by prohibiting the sale and manufacture of alcohol throughout the state. Once again, the men made their plans without consulting the WCTU, which doubted the likelihood of success but resolutely took on the task of circulating petitions to secure a place on the ballot for the proposal. The Temperance League formalized a coalition embracing representatives from allied Protestant denominations, but the United Drys organization confronted the well-funded Arkansas Against Prohibition (AAP) group. To counter the WCTU, the AAP appointed an east

Facing page:
A 1935 law authorized retail liquor stores but not the return of taverns or bars.

COURTESY OF SHILOH MUSEUM OF OZARK HISTORY.

Small Arkansas wineries emphasized local roots but remained an anathema to dry advocates.

Arkansas businesswoman to coordinate direct appeals to women but did not form an affiliated female association. At the same time, May C. Crouse, WCTU president, compromised her organization's independence both by becoming an officer in the United Drys and by urging members to promote the initiative through the churches rather than as white-ribboners. The antidrink forces relied upon the familiar technique of mass rallies to publicize their cause. A few days before the Nov. 7, 1950, election, a few hundred people gathered on the state Capitol steps to hear clergymen exhort the faithful to lead the nation back to the better days of Prohibition. The white choir members of the Ouachita Baptist University chanted "vote dry" while the African American students in the Arkansas Baptist College choir "sang hymns and spirituals."[8]

In contrast to the 1942 local option revision campaign, the voters clearly understood that approval of the 1950 proposal would impose prohibition. Opponents hammered home the point that the reduction in license fees and excise levies would either undermine services or force a tax increase. On the other hand, some dry supporters believed the act insufficiently stout. Following the advice of attorneys, Coulter attempted to insulate the proposal from legal challenges by bringing it in line with a 1947 measure that allowed individuals in dry localities to have a limited quantity of alcohol for personal consumption. Under Coulter's initiated act, individuals could still import and possess at least one quart of liquor. After the dry proposal was rejected 167,578 to 122,252, Coulter asserted that he had discovered compromise does not win over supporters: "In the future there will be no suggestion of one quart, or of even one thimbleful." While the United Drys leader believed in the ultimate triumph of the prohibition cause, savvy political observers knew that voters did not look back at Prohibition as a golden era. The experience had not matched the utopian claims of the temperance activists. Before the 1950 election, Gov. Sid McMath laconically voiced the common perception: "We tried prohibition once and everyone saw what happened." Privately, even some of the faithful believed they were fighting a losing battle. The day after Arkansans had soundly rejected the prohibition initiative, Jessie L. Knoll, WCTU secretary, wrote a disconsolate, cathartic rumination on the reasons for the loss: "People don't seem to have convictions or strong feelings anymore. Christians lean over backwards to be broadminded and tolerant. It is nearly noon, and none of our members have phoned to find out how I feel since our defeat. During the period I was sweating it out writing our cards—I was lonely, *so* lonely."[9]

Throughout the century, Arkansas business and industrial owners had been reluctant to climb aboard the temperance bandwagon. Prohibition always carried the prospect that revenue lost on alcohol sales might be recouped through other business taxes, and a dry state was harder to promote to outside investors and manufacturers. As the Arkansas economy began to take off after 1950 with a boom in food processing and clothing factories, the state government began to formalize economic development efforts. State officials also came to view tourism as an industry that could produce jobs without the expensive incentives attached to luring new manufacturers. Just as the legislature extended a helping hand to potential factory operations, it accommodated those interests that insisted visitors would expect cocktails to be available.[10]

In 1943 and in 1965, the General Assembly made it legal for customers to buy a bottle of beer to drink on premises and to have Arkansas wine served with a meal in a restaurant or hotel. The former chairman of the state's economic development commission and first Republican governor since the Reconstruction era, Winthrop Rockefeller, believed that authorizing local option elections for mixed drink sales would boost tourism and reform the inconsistent application of existing liquor laws. As was the case with nearly all of his proposals during two terms in office, Governor Rockefeller in May 1968 failed to move his initial mixed-drink proposal through an unfriendly Democratic legislature. However, the governor's own polling revealed overwhelming support for the change. He submitted a revised version of the measure for the regular 1969 session, but prospects remained uncertain.[11]

Legislators still disproportionately hailed from rural areas where local option elections had bounced liquor retailers. In addition, opponents objected that the act allowed mixed drinks to infiltrate dry counties. The proposed bill set up the procedures for holding elections on mixed-drink service in restaurants and hotels in wet locales, but it also authorized private clubs in dry communities to serve alcoholic concoctions without getting approval from officeholders or voters. Nevertheless, the days of organized temperance activism were past. The state WCTU, which would dissolve by the 1980s, was primarily a commemoration society and played no public role in the debate. The student newspaper at Ouachita Baptist University endorsed the measure as an honest response to hypocrisy and widespread evasion of existing laws. Representatives from the Arkansas Christian Civic Foundation testified at a Senate hearing that the bill was intended to grease the way for hotel expansion in Little Rock, a charge that was not disputed by the observers present from the Little Rock and Hot Springs chambers of commerce. Senator Melvin T. Chambers of Magnolia gave vent to the only expression of the old-style rhetoric: "The wrath of God is in Egypt today, and it's here, too." Making a hasty air trip from the National Governor's Council meeting in Washington, Governor Rockefeller signed the bill within three hours of its passage. With the governor's signature, the law

Gov. Winthrop Rockefeller pushed to loosen restrictions on drink sales to promote tourism and economic development.

COURTESY OF OLD STATE HOUSE MUSEUM.

took immediate effect and was less vulnerable to repeal through a petition drive for an initiated act.[12]

As the twentieth century drew to a close, even the local option battles cooled as the demarcation lines between wet and dry counties in Arkansas hardened. The forty-three dry counties were grouped primarily to the west of the thirty-two wet counties that dominated the delta region. Yet, even the cold war exacted costs to both camps, which still occasionally mounted campaigns to install or banish liquor outlets. Reflecting a general consensus that demon rum was no longer worth the fight, the legislature in 1985 and 1993 essentially revived the strictures from the 1935 act that had suppressed local option elections before the 1942 initiated law. The updated code required that petitions include the signatures of at least 38 percent of the voters before officials could organize elections, which were limited to once every four years. Senator Lu Hardin, the sponsor of the 1993 measure, made clear his intent: "This keeps communities from being polarized unnecessarily. There is nothing that polarizes a community like a wet-dry election."[13]

Nevertheless, battles flared on another front. Following the enactment of a 2003 measure that expanded the justification for forming private clubs to include "community hospitality, professional association, entertainment," the state Alcohol and Beverage Control board (ABC) granted private club licenses to restaurants in the otherwise dry communities of Batesville and Jonesboro (a number of nonprofit entities were already operating private clubs in both locales). The Jonesboro chamber of commerce director said that a town bereft of retail package stores but able to offer out-of-town business visitors a drink at a local club or café was the best of both worlds: "It's wet enough for the wets, and dry enough for the drys."[14]

A vocal group of drys, including groups and individuals associated with a variety of conservative social causes, did not agree. In April 2004, ministers and activists demanded at a public news conference that Gov. Mike Huckabee overhaul the ABC commission to insure that three of the five members hailed from dry counties. Huckabee, a Baptist minister who refused to serve alcohol during official functions at the governor's mansion, noted that he could not remove sitting commissioners under state law. Economic development boosters argued that a majority of Arkansans lived in wet counties. Bob Hester, head of American Family Association of Arkansas, was not mollified. In a May 2004 editorial, he charged that Huckabee ignored pleas from antialcohol leaders to be evenhanded in his ABC board appointments: "It is only fair for some people from dry counties to be put on the board, or at least for members to come to the table with an open mind."[15]

When it came to issues of fairness, John Barleycorn was always one to inspire strong opinions.

John Barleycorn and friends.

COURTESY OF OLD STATE HOUSE MUSEUM.

Notes

"John Barleycorn" was first published in a broadside in the early seventeenth century, during the reign of James I, although it was apparently already well-known throughout England and originated much earlier. The song describes a ritual in which the blood of the sacrificed folk figure, Barleycorn, waters the grain fields and strengthens those who eat the barley cakes. In keeping with the agricultural cycle, John Barleycorn continually returns to life. Robert Burns reworked the ballad in a 1782 poem and in the process transformed Sir John into the personification of alcoholic drink. This version of the original ballad appeared in the *Journal of Folk Song Society* Volume VIII, 41 (1937) and is reprinted at http://www.contemplator.com/england/jbcorn.html.

Chapter 1: Whiskey Battles on the Arkansas Frontier

1. Morris S. Arnold, *Colonial Arkansas, 1686–1804* (Fayetteville: University of Arkansas Press, 1991), 154; Kathleen DuVal, "The Education of Fernando De Lebya: Quapaws and Spaniards on the Border of Empires," *Arkansas Historical Quarterly* 60 (Spring 2001): 4–5.

2. DuVal, "De Lebya," 10; Arnold, *Colonial Arkansas,* 154; Morris S. Arnold, *The Rumble of a Distant Drum: The Quapaws and Old World Newcomers, 1673–1804* (Fayetteville: University of Arkansas Press, 2000), 90.

3. Arnold, *Distant Drum,* 150; Arnold, *Colonial Arkansas,* 155–56.

4. S. Charles Bolton, "Jeffersonian Indian Removal and the Emergence of Arkansas Territory," *Arkansas Historical Quarterly* 62 (Autumn 2003): 253–54; S. Charles Bolton, *Arkansas 1800–1860: Remote and Restless* (Fayetteville: University of Arkansas Press, 1998), 75–76.

5. Ed Bearss and Arrell M. Gibson, *Fort Smith: Little Gibraltar on the Arkansas* (Norman: University of Oklahoma Press), 116–17.

6. Secretary Joseph Browne to the President, July 8, 1806, in *Territorial Papers of the United States,* 26 vols., ed. Clarence Carter, (Washington, D.C.: Government Printing Office, 1934–69) vol. 13, 543n58; *Arkansas Gazette,* July 25, 1832; Bearss and Gibson, *Fort Smith,* 117–18; Odie B. Faulk and Billy Mac Jones, *Fort Smith: An Illustrated History* (Fort Smith: Old Fort Museum, 1983), 24–25; George H. Hunt,

"A History of the Prohibition Movement in Arkansas" (master's thesis, University of Arkansas, 1933), 13–14.

7. Bearss and Gibson, *Fort Smith,* 117–18; *Arkansas Gazette,* October 10, 1832; Hunt, "Prohibition Movement," 12. In 1838, the garrison returned and Fort Smith was reactivated.

8. W. J. Rorabaugh, *The Alcoholic Republic* (New York: Oxford University Press, 1979), 8, 61, 80–86; Henry Schoolcraft, *Rude Pursuits and Rugged Peaks: Schoolcraft's Ozark Journal, 1818–1819* (1821; repr., Fayetteville: University of Arkansas Press, 1996), 103; Ian R.Tyrrell, "Drink and Temperance in the Antebellum South: An Overview and Interpretation," *Journal of Southern History* 48 (November 1982): 505–6.

9. Friedrich Gerstacker, *Wild Sports in the Far West* (1854; repr., Durham, N.C.: Duke University Press, 1968), 163, 173–74; Hunt, "Prohibition Movement," 11; Lonnie J. White, *Politics on the Southwestern Frontier: Arkansas Territory, 1819–1836* (Memphis: Memphis State University Press, 1964), 29; *Arkansas Gazette,* May 14, 1828.

10. Gerstacker, *Wild Sports,* 173–74.

11. Thomas R. Pegram, *Battling Demon Rum: The Struggle for a Dry America, 1800–1933* (Chicago: Ivan R. Dee, 1998), 17–26; Ronald G. Walters, *American Reformers, 1815–1860* (New York: Hill and Wang, 1997), 129–32.

12. William F. Pope, *Early Days in Arkansas: Being For the Most Part the Personal Recollections of an Old Settler* (1895: repr., Easley, S.C.: Southern Historical Press, 1978), 108; Hunt, "Prohibition Movement," 8–9; Tyrell, "Temperance in South," 503.

13. Orville W. Taylor, *Negro Slavery in Arkansas* (1958: repr., Fayetteville: University of Arkansas Press, 2000), 113; *Acts of Arkansas, 1852–1853,* 71–72; *Arkansas Gazette,* February 6, 1828.

14. Charles F. M. Noland, *Pete Whetstone of Devil's Fork: Letters to the Spirit of the Times,* eds. Ted R. Worley and Eugene A. Nolte (Van Buren, Ark.: The Press-Argus, 1957), 9; Bolton, *Remote and Restless,* 110–12; Rorabaugh, *Alcoholic Republic,* 206–8.

15. Gerstäcker, *Wild Sports,* 372–73; Hunt, "Prohibition Movement," 24–27.

16. *Arkansas Gazette,* September 21, 1842, April 6, 1831; Hunt, "Prohibition Movement," 21–23; Jack S. Blocker Jr., *American Temperance Movements: Cycles of Reform* (Boston: Twayne, 1989), 11–14, 18–19, 21–22.

17. Kim Scott, "Window on the Frontier, 1840–1862: The Early Newspapers of Washington County, Arkansas," *Flashback* 38 (May 1988): 11–20; "Proceedings of the Fayetteville Temperance Society, 1841–1844, *Flashback* 32 (May 1982): 29.

18. Blocker, *Temperance Movements,* 26–27; Pegram, *Demon Rum,* 35–38.

19. *Arkansas Gazette,* October 5, 26, 1842; Walter N. Vernon, *Methodism in Arkansas, 1816–1976* (Little Rock: Joint Committee For the History of Arkansas Methodism, 1976), 31, 62–63.

20. *Acts of Arkansas, 1856–1857,* 31–32; Hunt, "Prohibition Movement," 29–31, 54; Pegram, *Demon Rum,* 40–42.

21. Tyrell, "Temperance in the South," 491–92, 509; Hunt, "Prohibition Movement," 23; Blocker, *Temperance Movements,* 48–51; Walters, *Reformers,* 132.

22. Mary Medearis, ed., *Sam Williams: Printer's Devil: Memorabilia: Some Ante Bellum Reminiscences of Hempstead County, Arkansas* (Hope, Ark.: Etter Printing Co., 1979), 156–57.

23. John Keet to James Graham, in *Authentic Voices: Arkansas Culture, 1541–1860,* ed. Sarah Fountain (Conway: University of Central Arkansas Press, 1986), 247–250.

Chapter 2: From Civil War to Moonshine Wars

1. Michael Dougan, *Confederate Arkansas: The People and Policies of a Frontier State in Wartime* (Tuscaloosa: University of Alabama Press, 1976), 96–98, 124.

2. Randy Finley, *From Slavery to Uncertain Freedom: The Freedmen's Bureau in Arkansas, 1865–1869* (Fayetteville: University of Arkansas Press, 1996), 51, 65–66.

3. *Acts of Arkansas, 1873,* 15–19; George H. Hunt, "A History of the Prohibition Movement in Arkansas" (master's thesis, University of Arkansas, 1933), 45–46; John William Graves, *Town and Country: Race Relations in an Urban-Rural Context, Arkansas, 1865–1905* (Fayetteville: University of Arkansas Press, 1990), 31. On Reconstruction in Arkansas see Thomas A. DeBlack, *With Fire and Sword: Arkansas, 1861–1874* (Fayetteville: University of Arkansas Press, 2003).

4. Various national and state laws are noted in Ernest H. Cherrington, *The Evolution of Prohibition in the United States of America* (Westerville, Ohio: American Issue Press, 1920).

5. Wilbur R. Miller, *Revenuers & Moonshiners. Enforcing Federal Liquor Law in the Mountain South, 1865–1900* (Chapel Hill: University of North Carolina Press, 1991), 16–31.

6. This description of the moonshining process is a distillation of a number of descriptions, although it owes much to Ernest Seaborn Pyle, *Punkin Center* (Magnolia, Ark.: 1997), 266–73, and to an unpublished paper in possession of the author that was written by Susan Young of the Shiloh Museum, Springdale, Arkansas.

7. Isaac Stapleton, *Moonshiners in Arkansas* (Independence, Mo.: Zion's Printing Company, 1920), 3; Miller, *Revenuers,* 80–81, 106–9.

8. Stapleton, *Moonshiners,* 16–18; *Arkansas Gazette,* February 8, 1898.

9. Stapleton, *Moonshiners,* 8–11.

10. Charles Morrow Wilson, *The Bodacious Ozarks: True Tales of the Backhills* (Gretna, La.: Pelican Publishing Company, 1959), 53; Otto Ernest Rayburn, "Moonshine Fact and Folklore" in "Rayburn's Folk Encyclopedia," Otto Ernest Rayburn Papers, Special Collections, University of Arkansas, Fayetteville; Otto Ernest Rayburn, *Ozark Country* (New York: Duell, Sloan and Pearce, 1941), 28.

11. Kenneth R. Hubbell, "Always a Simple Feast: Social Life in the Delta" in *The Arkansas Delta: Land of Paradox,* ed. Jeannie Whayne and Willard B. Gatewood (Fayetteville: University of Arkansas Press, 1993), 202; *Arkansas Gazette,* January 28, 1896; Miller, *Revenuers,* 16, 44; Jack Temple Kirby, *Rural Worlds Lost: The American South, 1920–1960* (Baton Rouge: Louisiana State University Press, 1987), 210.

12. Pyle, *Punkin Center,* 254, 277

13. O. C. Pill, interview by Bob Besom, January 1, 1990, Oral History Collection, Arkansas Museum of Natural Resources, Smackover; O. C. Pill, interview by Clara Ayres, August 4, 1989, Oral History Collection, Arkansas Museum of Natural Resources, Smackover.

Chapter 3: Prohibition Armies March to Victory

1. Ruth Bordin, *Woman and Temperance: The Quest For Power and Liberty, 1873–1900* (Philadelphia: Temple University Press, 1981), 19–22; Thomas R. Pegram, *Battling Demon Rum: The Struggle for a Dry America, 1800–1933* (Chicago: Ivan R. Dee, 1998), 45, 58–65; Nancy Britton, *Two Centuries of Methodism in Arkansas, 1800–2000* (Little Rock: August House, 2000), 145. Gaines M. Foster in *Moral Reconstruction: Christian Lobbyists*

and the Federal Legislation of Morality, 1865–1920 (Chapel Hill: University of North Carolina Press, 2002) argues that a tightly integrated moral lobby emerged in the 1870s that cooperated to push a moral reform program to stamp out drink, gambling, and other forms of commercial vice.

2. Nancy Woloch, *Women and the American Experience,* 3rd ed. (Boston: McGraw Hill, 2000), 203–4; Aileen S. Kraditor, *The Ideas of the Woman Suffrage Movement, 1890–1929* (Garden City, N.Y.: Doubleday, 1971), 46–48.

3. Pegram, *Demon Rum,* 67–72; Bordin, *Woman and Temperance,* 42–51, 57–58, 76–82. Carol Mattingly in *Well-Tempered Women: Nineteenth-Century Temperance Rhetoric* (Carbondale, Illinois: Southern Illinois University Press, 1998) explores how Willard and other WCTU leaders nurtured a conservative style based on decorum and evangelical rhetoric that was marshaled in service of progressive ends.

4. Henrietta Caldwell McQuiston, *History of the W.C.T.U. of Monticello* (n.p., 1920), 2–3; George H. Hunt, "A History of the Prohibition Movement in Arkansas" (master's thesis, University of Arkansas, 1933), 41–42; Thomas C. Kennedy, "The Rise and Decline of a Black Monthly Meeting: Southland, Arkansas, 1864–1925," *Arkansas Historical Quarterly* 50 (Summer 1991): 127–28.

5. Jessie Lowe Knoll, *A Partial Fruition: A History of the Woman's Christian Temperance Union of Arkansas* (Little Rock: Woman's Christian Temperance Union of Arkansas, 1951), 34–36; *Arkansas Gazette,* January 29, 1880.

6. *Woman's Chronicle,* March 23, 1889; 1888 state convention program, Woman's Christian Temperance Union Papers (hereafter cited as WCTU Papers), Series I, Box 2, File 1, University of Arkansas at Little Rock.

7. Hunt, "Prohibition Movement," 96–97; Knoll, *Partial Fruition,* 44; Bordin, *Woman and Temperance,* 135–38. The most recent study of temperance education is Jonathan Zimmerman, *Distilling Democracy: Alcohol Education in America's Public Schools, 1880–1925* (Lawrence: University Press of Kansas, 1999).

8. Fon Gordon, *Caste and Class: The Black Experience in Arkansas, 1880–1920* (Athens: University of Georgia Press, 1995), 93–94; Minutes and Year Book, Arkansas WCTU, 1916, Series 1, Box 3, File 2, WCTU Papers; Minutes and Year Book, Arkansas WCTU 1917, Series 1, Box 3,

File 3, WCTU Papers; Paul E. Isaac, *Prohibition and Politics: Turbulent Decades in Tennessee, 1885–1920* (Knoxville: University of Tennessee Press, 1965), 37; Bordin, *Woman,* 83–84; Pegram, *Demon Rum,* 71–72.

9. *Woman's Chronicle,* February 2, 13, 23, 1889; Elizabeth A. Taylor, "The Woman Suffrage Movement in Arkansas," *Arkansas Historical Quarterly* 15 (Spring 1956): 21–22, 28.

10. *Woman's Chronicle,* February 8, 1889; *Blackwell v. The State,* 36 *Arkansas Reports,* 184; *Acts of Arkansas, 1874–1875,* 206–207; *Acts of Arkansas, 1881,* 140–42; Hunt, "Prohibition Movement," 48–51.

11. *Woman's Chronicle,* September 15, 1888; *Acts of Arkansas, 1879,* 33–38.

12. Hunt, "Prohibition Movement," 85–86; Mike McNeill, "Here's Mud In Your Eye," *South Arkansas Sunday News,* August 12, 2001; Richard S. Daniels, "Blind Tigers and Blind Justice: The Arkansas Raid on Island 37, Tennessee," *Arkansas Historical Quarterly* 38 (Autumn 1979), 259–70; Sidney S. McMath, *Promises Kept: A Memoir* (Fayetteville: University of Arkansas Press, 2003), 33.

13. Hunt, "Prohibition Movement," 73–77; Carl H. Moneyhon, *Arkansas and the New South, 1874–1929* (Fayetteville: University of Arkansas Press, 1997), 81; Jack S. Blocker Jr., *American Temperance Movements: Cycles of Reform* (Boston: Twayne, 1989), 85–90.

14. *Woman's Chronicle,* August 4, September 28, 1888; Bordin, *Woman and Temperance,* 123–133.

15. *Arkansas Gazette,* February 16, 1906; Raymond Arsenault, *The Wild Ass of the Ozarks: Jeff Davis and the Social Bases of Southern Politics* (Knoxville: University of Tennessee Press, 1984), 143–49, 158–61; *Historical Report of the Secretary State, 1998,* 104–5; *Arkansas Gazette,* May 8, 1896.

16. Fran Grace, *Carry A. Nation, Retelling the Life* (Bloomington: Indiana University Press, 2001), 208–9, 262–74; *Arkansas Gazette,* February 17, 1906.

17. "Arkansas, History of Prohibition," George F. Thornburgh Scrapbook (hereafter cited as Thornburgh Scrapbook), Box 1, Folder 7, University of Arkansas Libraries, Fayetteville; *Arkansas Gazette,* March 1, April 5, 1894; Hunt, "Prohibition Movement," 72, 90; Austin K. Kerr, *Organized For Prohibition: A New History of the Anti-Saloon League* (New Haven, Conn.: Yale University Press, 1985), 67–81, 118–19; Blocker, *Temperance Movements,* 95–99.

18. *Western Methodist,* August 8, 1912; *Woman's Chronicle,* March 12, 1890; Pegram, *Demon Rum,* 91–98, 113–18.

19. *Arkansas Gazette,* September 21, 1908; Jo Ellen Maack (Old State House Museum), "Behind Closed Doors: The Inside Story of the Villa Marre," unpublished paper in possession of author.

20. Arsenault, *Wild Ass,* 15; "Arkansas," Box 1, Folder 6, Thornburgh Scrapbook; Thomas R. Pegram, "Temperance Politics and Regional Political Culture: The Anti-Saloon League in Maryland and the South, 1907–1915," *Journal of Southern History* 58 (February 1997) : 80–81.

21. *Arkansas Gazette,* January 9, 1909; "Great is Diana of the Ephesians," clipping, Box 1, Folder 4, Thornburgh Scrapbook; *Western Methodist,* September 19, 1907; *Baptist Advance,* August 22, 1907.

22. Calvin R. Ledbetter, *Carpenter from Conway: George Washington Donaghey as Governor of Arkansas, 1909–1913* (Fayetteville: University of Arkansas Press, 1993), 130–31; "Copy of Petition for Initiated Act," Box 1, Folder 5, Thornburgh Scrapbook; David M. Moyers, "Arkansas Progressivism: The Legislative Record" (PhD diss., University of Arkansas, 1986), 254–55; Hunt, "Prohibition Movement," 121–22. On the relationship of temperance to southern Progressivism see William A. Link, *The Paradox of Southern Progressivism, 1880–1930* (Chapel Hill: University of North Carolina Press, 1992) and Dewey W. Grantham, *Southern Progressivism: The Reconciliation of Progress and Tradition* (Knoxville: University of Tennessee Press, 1983).

23. Richard L. Niswonger, *Arkansas Democratic Politics, 1896–1920* (Fayetteville: University of Arkansas Press, 1990), 200–201; Knoll, *Partial Fruition,* 52; *Arkansas Methodist,* August 29, October 3, 1912; Hunt, "Prohibition Movement," 132–34; Moyers, "Progressivism," 256; *Arkansas Gazette,* September 9, 19, 1912.

24. Arsenault, *Wild Ass,* 214; Moyers, "Arkansas Progressivism," 257; Ledbetter, *Carpenter from Conway,* 130–31. The proposed amendment would have required that voters who would have been ineligible to vote on January 1, 1866, submit to a literacy exam, *Arkansas Gazette,* September 7, 1912.

25. *McClure v. Topf & Wright, 112 Arkansas Reports,* 342–54; Hunt, "Prohibition Movement," 135–38; Jeannie Whayne, *A New Plantation South: Land, Labor, and Federal Favor in Twentieth Century Arkansas* (Charlottesville: University of Virginia Press, 1996), 28, 32–37.

26. *Acts of Arkansas, 1915,* 98–100; *Arkansas Gazette,* February 6, 17,

1915; Niswonger, "George Washington Hays," in *The Governors of Arkansas,* 2nd ed., Timothy P. Donovan, Willard B. Gatewood, Jr,, and Jeannie M. Whayne, eds. (Fayetteville: University of Arkansas Press, 1995), 141.; Hunt, "Prohibition Movement," 140–43.

27. Hunt, "Prohibition Movement," 145; *Arkansas White Ribboner,* Novemeber 20, 1917; Moyers, "Progressivism," 258–73.

28. Pegram, *Demon Rum,* 144–49; Hunt, "Prohibition Movement," 146–50. In 1918 the Arkansas Supreme Court ruled that under the "bone dry law" private individuals as opposed to commercial carriers could legally bring liquor into the state. The 1919 legislature, which ratified the Eighteenth Amendment, also passed a measure to close this loophole in the 1917 act.

Chapter 4: The Dry Kingdom Under Assault

1. Frances. M. Ross, "The New Woman as Club Woman and Social Activist in Turn of the Century Arkansas," *Arkansas Historical Quarterly* 50 (Winter 1991): 343, 345; Jessie Lowe Knoll, *A Partial Fruition: A History of the Woman's Christian Temperance Union of Arkansas* (Little Rock: Woman's Christian Temperance Union of Arkansas, 1951), 63–71; *Arkansas White Ribboner,* 20 Nov. 1917; Minutes and Yearbook of WCTU of Arkansas, 1919, Box 3, File 3, WCTU Papers.

2. W. David Baird, "Thomas Jefferson Terral" in *The Governors of Arkansas,* 160–64; Ernest Seaborn Pyle, *Punkin Center* (Magnolia, Ark.: 1997), 264.

3. Charles C. Alexander, *The Ku Klux Klan in the Southwest* (Lexington: University of Kentucky Press, 1965), 217–18; Charles C. Alexander, "White Robed Reformers: the Ku Klux Klan Comes to Arkansas," *Arkansas Historical Quarterly* 22 (Spring 1963), 8–23; Kathleen M. Blee, *Women of the Klan* (Berkeley: University of California Press, 1991), 88–89.

4. Alexander, *Ku Klux Klan in Southwest*, 76–77; A. R. and R. B. Buckalew, "The Discovery of Oil in South Arkansas, 1920–1924," *Arkansas Historical Quarterly* 33 (Autumn 1974), 225, 235.

5. *Arkansas Gazette,* November 31, 1922; *Arkansas Gazette,* August 11, 12, 20, 1925; Donald Holley, "A Look Behind the Masks: The 1920s Ku Klux Klan in Monticello, Arkansas," *Arkansas Historical Quarterly* 60 (Summer 2001): 141–142, 145.

6. David E. Kyvig, *Repealing National Prohibition* (Chicago:

University of Chicago Press, 1979), 92, 120–26; Jack S. Blocker Jr., *American Temperance Movements: Cycles of Reform* (Boston: Twayne, 1989), 124–27.

7. *Arkansas White Ribboner,* September 1928; Michael Richard Strickland, "Rum, Rebellion, Racketeers, and Rascals: Alexander Copeland Millar and The Fight to Preserve Prohibition in Arkansas, 1927–1933" (master's thesis, University of Arkansas, Fayetteville, 1993), 53–66; Cecil Edward Weller, Jr., *Joe T. Robinson: Always a Loyal Democrat* (Fayetteville: University of Arkansas Press, 1998), 109–21.

8. Kyvig, *Repealing Prohibition,* 171–78.

9. *Arkansas White Ribboner,* September 1933; Strikland, "Millar," 101–12.

Chapter 5: Cold War: Conflict and Coexistence

1. *Acts of Arkansas, 1933,* 19–35. In April 1933, Congress revised the Volstead Act to legalize 3.2 percent beer as the repeal of the Eighteenth Amendment went forward.

2. J. R. Morris, "The Wine and Juice Industry in Arkansas," *American Wine Society Journal* 29 (1997): 94–96. Robert Cowie of the Arkansas Wine Museum provided crucial background on the state's wine industry.

3. *Arkansas Gazette,* January 26, February 5, 1935; C. Calvin Smith, "Junius Marion Futrell" in *The Governors of Arkansas,* 181; Ben F. Johnson, *Arkansas In Modern America, 1930–1999* (Fayetteville: University of Arkansas Press, 2000), 17.

4. *Acts of Arkansas, 1935,* 258–99; *Arkansas Gazette,* February 26, March 6, 8–10, 1935.

5. *Arkansas Gazette,* November 3, 1942.

6. E. Glenn Hinson, *A History of Baptists in Arkansas, 1818–1978* (Little Rock: Arkansas State Convention, 1979), 287–88; *Arkansas Gazette,* October 25, 1942; Jessie Lowe Knoll, *A Partial Fruition: A History of the Woman's Christian Temperance Union of Arkansas* (Little Rock: Woman's Christian Temperance Union of Arkansas, 1951), 81; *Arkansas White Ribboner,* March 1942, June 1942.

7. *Arkansas Gazette,* February 4, 1950; Jack S. Blocker Jr., *American Temperance Movements: Cycles of Reform* (Boston: Twayne, 1989), 138–39; Knoll, *Partial Fruition,* 87.

8. *Arkansas Gazette*, September 7, November 5, 1950; *Arkansas White Ribboner,* April 1950; Knoll, *Partial Fruition* 88.

9. Jessie Knoll, "Written Day After the Election," note, Box 5, File 1, WCTU Papers; *Arkansas Democrat,* [Feb. 1950], clipping, Box 5, File 1, WCTU Papers; *Arkansas Gazette,* November 9, 11, 14, 1950.

10. Johnson, *Modern Arkansas,* 111–19.

11. *Acts of Arkansas, 1943,* 512–18; *Acts of Arkansas, 1965,* 326–31; *Acts of Arkansas, 1969,* 384–403. Section 1 of the 1969 act included the following rationale: "The General Assembly determines that the tourist and convention industry contributes substantially to the revenues of business enterprises in this State and that income from the tourist trade, conventions and allied industries is essential to the continued well-being and prosperity of this State."

12. *Arkansas Gazette,* February 27–28, March 1, 1969; Cathy Kunzinger Urwin, *Agenda For Reform: Winthrop Rockefeller as Governor of Arkansas, 1967–71* (Fayetteville: University of Arkansas Press, 1991), 121–23.

13. *Acts of Arkansas, 1985,* 423; *Acts of Arkansas, 1993,* 430; *Arkansas Democrat-Gazette,* January 27, 1993.

14. *Arkansas Democrat-Gazette*, March 14, 2003; *Acts of Arkansas, 2003,* 6959.

15. *Arkansas Democrat-Gazette,* March 14, April 21, May 23, 2004.

Index